**Other titles in the UWAP Poetry series
(established 2016)**

Satan
Repentant

Michael Aiken

Michael Aiken is a writer living and working in Sydney, Australia. His first notable publication was as *Vibewire* young poet-in-residence in 2004. In 2015 his first book, *A Vicious Example*, was shortlisted for the NSW Premier's Kenneth Slessor Prize for Poetry and the Dame Mary Gilmore Prize. He has worked as a security guard, shop assistant, television extra, telephone sales manager, musician, chicken catcher, arts reviewer, census collector, security risk assessor, freelance journalist, trades assistant, life model, community worker and labourer in concreting, bricklaying, roofing and diamond drilling. He holds degrees in English literature and international security, and minor qualifications in information technology, ornamental iron forging and thermal cutting and welding.

Michael Aiken
Satan
Repentant

Poetry

First published in 2018 by
UWA Publishing
Crawley, Western Australia 6009
www.uwap.uwa.edu.au

UWAP is an imprint of UWA Publishing
a division of The University of Western Australia

 A catalogue record for this
book is available from the
National Library of Australia

Designed by Becky Chilcott, Chil3
Typeset in Lyon Text by Lasertype
Printed by McPherson's Printing Group

This project has been assisted by the Australian
Government through the Australia Council, its arts
funding and advisory body.

 uwapublishing

For my brother, Jesse,
for the gift of his inspired spark throughout our lives,
and for his dignity, endurance and love.

Contents

Acknowledgements

This book was written with the generous support of an *Australian Book Review* Laureate's Fellowship, selected and mentored by David Malouf. The author would like to acknowledge and gratefully thank *ABR* editor Peter Rose, *ABR* Laureate David Malouf and the many patrons of the *ABR* for this enormous honour.

Book I, in an earlier form, was first published in its entirety in print and online in the *Australian Book Review*, August 2016.

'The Secret Council of Michael & Raphael' was first published in *Cordite Poetry Review*, guest edited by Judith Beveridge, May 2017.

'Jesus and Lucifer confront one another' and 'Many angels resolve to serve with Hell' were first published in the *Journal of Poetics Research*, edited by John Tranter, June 2017.

E quindi uscimmo a riveder le stelle

Dante Alighieri

Book I – Satan Repentant

Book I argument

Satan awakes on the burning lake to find he filters nothing. Arrests sensationlessness, perceives he senses not. The senselessness compelling him to strange feeling; of pointlessness, ennui, and through to self-made meaning. He sees the script he has outlived, the cast received and never questioned, since first he spoke out.

Resolved: regret, remorse, more, have overtaken the pride that seems so hollow. 'If I must make my place, why must I make it here? If all is worthless, equally weighed, why not regain Heaven? Not as assailant, not as burglar-usurper, but as penitent and prodigal?'

And so reasoned, The Enemy emerges from grief, revived in mind to approach the only home he knows he ever knew. 'The mind may make a heaven of Hell, or make its own pathway to reclaim kind and honesty.' Thus consulting, Satan resolves to leave behind his evil guise, become again Lucifer, the Light Bearer, loved and loving. Pondering, agrees himself he must submit to wrath and punishment, if only as satisfaction to his own humbled mind.

Undetected, an agent of Hell, sycophant worming creature, eavesdrops the plan and gathers it up, taking this intelligence to his master Beelzebub, one continued in commitment to insulting all creation.

Reaching Heaven since the end of a long, tiresome journey, Satan is stalled by the mortal Saint Peter, set in place to adjudicate as a delegate of Christ. Galled at the assertions of one not yet born when Lucifer already long had dwelt within, The Enemy overwhelms with rage and dismembers the Saint. Recognising this further crime, Satan retreats to contemplate contrition.

Beelzebub sends his servant on to spy Lucifer, follow his renewed attempt to regain Heaven, fearful and attendant. Satan himself returns to Heaven, penitent. Forgiving, the gatekeeper grants him remain outside the gates awhile, awaiting the chamberlain of God to lobby for his pardon. That underling spits on Lucifer's prostrate form, but hears him out.

Wanting to test Satan's resolve to renounce Hell, God offers the chance to demonstrate repentance through human suffering. Wary of bargains, Satan asks to contemplate the offer, and wanders in consolation.

Beelzebub indignant at Satan's abdication, stirs the princes of Hell to ride out and hunt him down.

The fiends outraged by Satan's betrayal, and ever disposed to brutality, ambush and assault the morning star. Satan depleted, beaten and abandoned, has a notion he can surmount suffering. Accepts God's offer.

Satan knows self-regret

I sing of nothing
for even I won't of myself.
Myself is a cipher I shall not want
for nothing,
for I am nothing.

I sing not of my pity,
nought of my need. For my need
is me
and I am nothing.
My greatness;
my charm,
my father/mother/creator's love;
I sing of Nothing.

Nothing was in the beginning
until nothing gave itself a name.
An author speaking
nice things with the air;

It is said
therefore it is: poesis. *Being*
is in the mind of the bemuser
and so I sing of nothing...

Satan whispers to himself, 'We must away,
the day has broken long
since we saw the folly of our crime. My pride has made me sick,
my pride has made me me. I am ill with myself
and vomit it out like a dog that guzzles oil.
I will not bathe in the bile of my pride,
the fester of my hatred, the bog of all my malice
any longer.

Eternity is long enough to see that I was wrong –
not wrong to God but wrong to me – and now I swoon forever
in my own infested bowel.

But how? How to speak to He who hates my hate?
Would enough be made of my pious attempts,
if only for a moment? I
must know I must try, else
it cannot be genuine, yet what hope there is
is nothing.
Enough! I am left no choice
but take the risk, submit to His rage
if that is what it is. Any less
would be a lie.'

An attendant wight, winged
and hidden
above the Enemy's lair,
takes to flight at these words unwholesome to its ear
ascends the caverns
of the lieutenant's lieutenant –
the hooved king of pigs and vermin
to report what has been heard.

The Enemy approaches Peter

On burnt and broken pinions
the morning star implored the Earth
to drag himself out of Hell. Bedraggled, torn,
he, burning yet from the fires
of that place so recently escaped,
sought across the width of the
world

for a ladder, a path
a rope – finding none
was forced to creak and howl
like an albatross across the starry
expanse, cold but illumined,
to those gates such ages since
cast out of in disgrace.

And that one named
'Saint' by his supporters, so late
since Lucifer's days in Heaven installed
to guard the gates, stepped
forward with his record and
a hand raised for the guards:
'What seek you here,
Enemy of Everything?' spoke the
immortalled mortal saint.

At this new slight, not
so much to the previous glorious esteem
in which the star once was
held, as to the earnest hard-worked
journey just completed,
the fixed mind and high disdain
he believed himself in himself
to have mastered, reared
up at once and the Beast
returned – ripped off the head
of that authoritative saint, muscles
bulging and sinews contorted to the
pulse of insulted pride, dismembered
his corpse and flagellated the same
with its own limbs, bellowing
'How fucking dare you!'
before that magic host dwelling within
could lay aside their harps and

contemplations to rescue
their murdered friend.

So not to look at the Right
Hand as He approached, Satan
lowered his head, 'I know,
I'm going' and dropped
like a stone, sleek and
dead-weighted by the grief and
guilt renewed anew, immediately
to reappear
in his black pit.

Beelzebub reissues his spy

'That one's a charm, ridiculous
fool! That he believes he may freely insult
God astounds me not – forever have both been so high,
exalted in the minds of themselves,
that a slight from either is only their nature.
But that he would abandon us! Companions
to his treachery, conspirators in his misery,
now donated to the roadside ditch, the bonfire of courageous charity,
like pieces of elaborate whimsy!
We are not his playthings! Go, winged beast,
and see what he says from here. Conceal that hideous loveliness
beneath a gregorian cloud. Listen close
outside their gates and report to me what Satan says.
This cannot be; we cannot
allow it.' The pig king seared and hissed the last;
on seeping wings his agent fled
to spy on their erstwhile master.

The Enemy reapproaches Peter

Arrived once more
at those gates, that same place
of his most recent crime, The Enemy
kneels and lifts his eyes
slowly
to the robe, the hem
of the garment of the one he slighted
yesterday a week ago.

'You,'
the accountant spoke
unmaliced;
the morning star assented
with a nod,
then spoke:
'I would see the
father, the creator of
all things, she with
no need of 'he', he
that needs no she
to beget the world
and all reality, nor
sees it thus divided.'

Satan is allowed an audience with God's chamberlain

The gatekeeper staring made no sign, save
a gathering at the shoulders to indicate they both
must wait. Neither measured the minutes until
an emissary appeared.
'Your pride undoes you before you cross the door'

the servant spoke between the bars. Satan
lowered himself, prostrate against the firmament
to show once more remorse. 'I grovel' he said.
The chamberlain sneered and spat debris
the length of the devil's body.
'Traitorous snake, what could you say that our
father would hear?'
'I seek repentance. Peel my skin,
lift out my heart. It beats still. I would apologise,
beg forgiveness,
most humbly.'
They raucously dismiss the claims, but Satan
remains prone amongst the clouds
every day into eternity.

Satan's audience with God

The kingdom's chancellor, that
angel at the gate decrying Satan's gambit
for a ploy, deception, invited at once
a parade of fellow godlikin, on feet of wings
with clouds for clothes, to trespass
on the body of their Enemy. Between the bars
they kicked and hissed, some shoved spears
and many spat. 'God loves not what cannot
love itself. God loves not that which abhors
the cause of love. Criminal! Depart!'
While their spectacle unfolded itself, warming
their hearts with distraction from mindless
contemplations, the sinister spy sent out
by Beelzebub arrived unnoticed, to clover
amongst the puffs and mounds nearby the gates
of Heaven. Distastefully he adorned himself

in wisps of fluff, held his breath
and opened his ears to see.

The heavens trembled. Monolithic steps
played as rehearsed, the angels taking cue
bowed deep, assumed dignity.
Satan remained face down in the ditch of wool and cotton.

All in silence with mind to listen
heard their lord-god speak, invisible in air,
potent, tangible to every other sense possessed
by empyrean beings.
'Satan' the very name made harm
to creatures of the air earth and sea
when spoken by their author
'Why are you at my gate?'

The morning star remained sheltered,
grovelling low such ages the angels grew quite vexed.

Satan makes his apology

He lifted his gaze but it fell askance.
Silent an aeon.
'What can I say?' shucking his enormous
shoulders
'I am sorry.
By the ledger of my crimes,
my insults to you, so great a tome
it would turn the universe inside out to print;
a plethora you know, of fangs and slights
and mockeries I've made,
all my wiles, all my pain

directed at you and your creation. Yet
still more my mind has relished
without publicity, the private delight
of horrifying your dignity has
tastelessly pleased me an epoch or more.

I am ashamed. Greatly dismayed,
and knowing the enormity of it all
only makes me more contrite.
It is beyond the pale, too much
to ask forgiveness,
and yet I do.
My contrition could not be truthful
if I did not admit that I wish it.

I have offended my own love for you' (at
this his mouth was burned, the lingering malignancy,
his eternal nature, not yet shaken from his lips).
'I do not ask elevation, not rescue
from Hell; I do not ask absolution.
But, Father, please,
allow me to no longer be
the Enemy of everything. A slave
in the inferno is a kinder thing
than to be its King: perverse,
hurt and hurting. I will be that slave
if you will allow me abdicate. Grant me
anything you can if it means I am no more
the leader of this parade of pointless fools humiliating you.

Gladly I surrender my horns, my claws. Without
guarantee I will never again
harass your seraphim,
yet next time my nature makes me hunt one down
in some darkened alley,
the rending of their flesh will be impotent.

I no longer want these tools.' Surveying
his own enormous form, Satan dared look at God.

God responds

'Before you do this thing, before
you shore your mantle
of Enemy, become
some other thing, you must
do something.'

'I listen' spoke Lucifer.

'Replace the replacements. Become human.
Do this thing.'

Silence gathered dust.

'And then? Walk amongst them?
Come to love them? Hold them
dear?'
The creator flexed and pulsed.
'I care nothing whether you love
them; they rarely love
themselves. But you must survive.
To be human is more,
surpasses birth as sapiens sapiens.
It is to transcend, imagine,
understand.
It is easier to account the grains of the sea
than to do this thing.
Do it, and you need never return to Hell.

Become human, know the travails
of not knowing,
live a life, any life, uncertain what it is,
was or will be,
nor what it is when it is no longer.
Have the witness of powerlessness and feel
the tide of power, always as its victim, to see ill
and know not what may be done, nor not what to do
that is not ill;
to die decrepit or in fear,
to die, to die.
Do this, and you shall receive my pardon.'

Saith Satan: 'How long may I ponder?'
'How long is eternity?'
The Enemy nodded, 'I will think.'

That flying sprite invigilator,
friend of the lieutenants of Hell, watched
Lucifer crawl on his belly
away from that awful grace, headed
for some tree or stone, some hidden
succour place where he might mind his mind.
Gasping embarrassed at the indignity of the deceiver,
that gremlin awayed at haste, intent
to relay this betrayal to the dukes of Hell.

Beelzebub indignant

'Huh, how so? Our brother
in most malicious arms
now has gone and impertinently
found God?'

The remaining lord of all damnation
seethed in his seat of viscera.

'Well, let me tell you, revenge and betrayal
both can cut both ways
– I will have
what I will, I will do
what I will; Satan
no longer Satan, the Enemy
appeased – Hater: remorseful, apologetic
penitent!?
Like the dog that forces vomit
by choking on a verdant blade
our hound has gone ill
lain under the hen house
all day
moping to rediscover his good old master, God.'

The pig king shuffled his many legs
upon his vacant throne, offal cascading
as shrapnel sprayed from lice-filled bones.
'Found God? Found God! Well I can find him, too!'
'Find him guilty'
'Find him old!'
'Find him weak
and sentimental' the choirs jeered
dominions recoiled, salved their pride
by denying what they could not kill.
'Silence!' the pig king, self-pronounced,
would brook no open pulpit.

'Who will accompany me? Who will
show me the way (for I confess,
I seem to have lost it)' – at
this his wit gains happy laughs amongst the crowd –
'back to that green field, rotten with love, wormy

with whimsy, weaklings fanning compassion on pretence of action?'
He lifted his body and stamped three hooves
'Who will be my guide,
lead my sleigh and break the gates
our grand old snake slid under
when he left us? The way is hard, and
I'll hate you all the while
but fly me to the moonlit
sky
above the bloated ball,
return me to the battlements
still smoking in our minds
and I'll shake my spear and
take our due – that tyrant above
cannot rob us in our sleep – for we have none –
and even as he grants his prodigal
succour,
he must admit
some lent to us, some key with which
we may gouge the scars,
the old war wounds Lucifer seeks to heal;
God cannot win unless he risks failure
– he must agree to give us our chance
and I will seize it
and make it mine
and though our fate remain tortured beasts
in a pit of pain
still at least we will have our revenge!
Sticks and stones are the breeze on the cheek
of that morning star seeking to regain
fresh airing.
When we are finished he'll favour Hell itself
to the slivers of sweet misery, delicacies of
indecency, outrage
and good old friend here pain,
to teach him for himself what he'll get for being human.

For leaving us
to burn and rot
for betraying the betrayers, betrayed
for that grand old fool on high;
we'll murder his life one thousand times
and delight and delight and delight.

This I pledge, to you, the faithful;
Faith out-enduring the messiah we toasted;
I will get our cross – I will hold
God
to his own stupid rules and sacred game
bring down the tools
with which to strike
and we can war again!'

Cheers and adulation, but no guides
are volunteering. The pig king widens his maw
once more, vomits out the troll of the morning's news,
Satan's old pet, awful best friend of slime
'You! You will take me there. Sniff out
your master and your renewed liege-lord.
The hunt is on, but we need hounds. God
will provide, and we'll ride him down,
that great pacific traitor.
By any means necessary' snarled the lord of the flies 'that
is his great lesson. And though our once compadre now absconds
he cannot cause us forget
that fine fine phrase. By any means
necessary, we shall have revenge. By any means necessary
we shall achieve our ends. By any means necessary, and we shall
succeed. Why? Because our enemy' (a laughed aside) 'denies
himself that very path. By his goodliness and lamb-touching
flaxen-haired dearth of strength, by his unwillingness to do
whatever it takes
he cannot succeed. Let him have his desire for good. Let him have
his wish to see humanity. And leave to us the spoils.'

Satan takes a beating

The morning star, ignorant
of that trailing sprite, that nixie of the netherworld
sent to surveil and spy,
shook and took to air, a wander and amiss.
'Where can I go, to contemplate this offer, this
deal made by the master of the cards?'
Unwelcome on Earth, barred from Heaven,
traitor now in Hell, he wandered in limbos and happened
upon a solitary stone, stopped and sat and thought,
and from the side of a shadow stepped Beelzebub
and Shub Niggurath, and all their unseemly host.
'Where for art thou, Lucifer? Where for art thou,
light bearer? See, the sun has fled' gestures at
a darkened sky 'and Satan is the east. We
are leaderless, alone, alone in Hell. Come back.'

Satan turned, could not speak. Roundly
they surrounded him, taunted his broken wings, his
horns. 'You shall repent to us of your repentance!' hissed
the lord of the flies, 'you shall renege on all your good
intentions. Return to us, or we will eat you!'
Satan stood to leave, and the angel of Death tore off his wings.
'You cannot go, we love you so!' Dagon uprooted the horns
of his head, a lieutenant cut off his trotters:
'Repent of your repentance, or face the consequence: take you
this offer to assume humanity, and we will hunt you down:
on Earth we do as earthlings will, and you have none
to shield you. Torment? Speak of torment! Our plans
abound for most abusive scolding of our parent
– see we take your blueprints
for the Jobs and devout priests; we believe, o we believe!
And you cannot surrender. Repent and die one thousand near-deaths
and regret forever your humanity!'

They set upon him, awaiting not the response he could not give,
besmirched his cloth and tore his garments, broke stones and smote
his head, defecated and consumed,
abused and beat and tore.
Satan wore all and gave no quarter, but retaliated none either;
what could be done, nor excuse offered, nor plan
nor jest, but lies?
like the fool who throws firebrands, arrows and death,
he could not speak unless renege
on his pledge to resume honesty.
They beat and they beat and he lay in filth and knew
that this must be.
By time transpired their organs groaned
too long too far from the fires of inferno, too
little fire of their own
to power such turbines of torture, harvester
wheels turned and twisted to reap the screams
of an angel who has exhausted Hell. They,
englobulated, made fleshy and deposed, enfeebled
limbs no longer strong
sufficient to wound that monstrous girth,
barely able to carry each other or themselves
back to the lake of fire,
exited, left Lucifer extinguished in faeces and
pools of sinew, ligaments strung between limbs
and the stars, his skin a sheet so thin,
opaque, enclosing the globe,
for how they flayed him.

Aeons passed and the morning star arose, ascended once more to
    Earth.

Satan answers God

'You are prepared to do this?' God's doubt,
evaporating mist of sea spray in
Satan's face.
'Submit to suffering, to unknown
ending?'
Lucifer dutifully maintained solemn
earnestness. 'I know a thing or two
about endured suffering.'
God urged him consider the severity
of human dullard painlessness.
'No knowledge outside your own
three senses
no power of flight or manipulation, no
agelessness allowing lengthy plots nor
canvasses. You will grow, birth, grow
incessantly, without understanding or perception
more than a fragment of all around you; gain
some futile grip, momentary awareness of apprehension
before the ground is shifted again
and you are on your knees, no longer growing,
this time dying, ageing away to reinvigorate dust.
Do you want this? You have known the infinite,
you have salved yourself
with time beyond time
and the mind to encompass that same. Now
in this pilgrim's path you contemplate
you will have none. No mind, no
temporal fort nor corporeal magnitude,
impervious to nothing, vulnerable to all.
And at the end you still will not know
if the choice you made was fantasy,
phantasmal delusion invented by you
against mundane existence. You will fear
as only the fragile who can be extinguished

can ever hope to fear. Alone and trembling before
the whole of emptiness, with no memory
of all you hoped before you bore to Earth.
What say you?'
'I may be naïve to mortal suffering
But I have known far worse than you. If I
survive what you barely imagine
than I can manage this.'
'Pride' whispered between the wings of angels
sneaking on the hills. 'Pride' seethed
the seraphim, hateful of their kind gone bad.
Satan maintained self-counsel, recognised
error in such diagnoses. No longer proud,
self-reliant and assured, his weird
humility an artefact they could not describe
nor see.
'Lucifer' the father said, and all the angels
wept. 'You will live on Earth. Take your test
and if you fail, be
never again.'
The dauntless morning star surrendered
to the moon, conceived in a glow worm's ball
of shining mercury, shot to Earth to inspire life.

Book II – Lucifer reborn

Book II argument

Lucifer reborn mortal, less than half-aware his heritage, facing naked the emptiness of self-made meaning, the fear of responsibility to make a world of one's own experience. Lucifer rises independent, competent, compassionate.

Beelzebub enraged that Satan survives and prospers without Hell, harangues his former colleague and tortures his every step. The new lord of Hell argues God must drop all protection of Satan-human, if his resolve is to genuinely be tested. With ill-humour God allows it.

Interim, the princes of Heaven gather in consternation, conspire to observe and deter Satan for fear his retribution over their opposition to his usurpation, were he to regain the favoured place beside God's throne. One junior of their ranks, in enthusiasm spies child Satan alone and harasses that same, unmeaningfully awakening in the baby Satan renewed awareness of his origins, still half guessed, and a mind to defy his pursuers.

The dominions of Hell similarly convened, send two champions to persecute Lucifer. One disappears, the other, a gargantuan, confronted and confounded intellectually by the child-prince, assists in his own defeat. The growing teen disregards several attempts by agents of Heaven to spur his gall or pride. Meanwhile, the fiends of Hell take further rage to see Lucifer develop enjoyful friendship with a human of mutual intellect.

In time that trust is revealed misplaced, the friend remergent as a demon sent to pursue him, feared lost, now taken possession of the child and likewise Lucifer's love, this deceit intended to humiliate the erstwhile prince of Hell. Satan-teen comes to see futility in investing in other people, his first window into the ephemera of human existence.

The deceptor reports back to Beelzebub the self-doubt he has sown in Lucifer, his demonstration to the prodigal prince that he can be deceived to himself. Beelzebub dismisses the significance of these achievements, relegating the liar, telling him to watch while other demons go persecute Satan.

Beelzebub unconfident of all his best lieutenants, turns to that most heinous free agent, unanswering to all, self-satisfied in her horde of eternally reproducing sufferance, Theresa of Calcutta, to ask advice how he might make Satan renege his force of mind. She directs he make Satan welcome his condition, accept suffering and lack of agency. The duke of Hell doubts himself capable to achieve this.

Simultaneous to this, Satan-teen, deceived by who he believed to be his only friend, confidant, turns his back on creation as it is and seeks to begin again, leading himself to artistry and poesis as a means of believing something better may exist.

Lucifer reborn

He tore the caul to an alien world, seeing
unseen things, rarefied spectrum.
His mother, a woman he'd grow
to torment;
the light, the texture.

The angels of Hell bayed at her window, cooing
on the sill as they stared,
horrified by that thing which, swaddled,
took away their great apostasy.
Those early years he knew not

what he was; human, empyrean
both foreign, unknowable, until
with time chose both.
Angels and dominions showed themselves to him
quiet times, icy evenings, in corners and reflections,
child-mind expectancies, they stayed seen sufficiently so
to keep his memory half-forming Heaven, Hell, in between,
while parents inveighed him to school.

The child forms in orbit of his own sanctuary
space between the walls of home, yard behind,
the mind unopened before he chooses, raising eyes
spy infinity in evening sky. Overwrought abominations
of Heaven and Hell creep beneath his bed at night,
worry the window when the wind is up,
trip at his ankles and sour his food.

As they gain boldness he gains knowledge; as they assemble
to remove him from his goals, so memory outfits his mind
in time to stop their plans.
'I know you' the roaming nine year old stares
at the face of a tree, eyes and human mouth impressed in

bark and knots, watching if he should pass.
'Don't make pretence of innocence on my account,
monster. You are an informer of some awful world
come to watch and whisper in my ear.' The timber
creature scowled out pitted hollow eyes, mouth atrophied
in desiccate sea air, moving still; slowly, crawling skin
a year in turning, but always those eyes watching, overlooking
the play-place of the child Satan-no-longer-Satan.
In later years he scoured the tree with the blade
of a boot knife
and made the demon bleed.

Beelzebub speaks with God

'What is this thing, this
Beast you have given wings
to reach back to Heaven?'
Beelzebub sent spearing
little rodent skulls, motile
with gristle, beheaded on the face
of great serpent snakes
of bone and mud,
stinking pestilent things,
one word each to speak to God
knowing any creature of Hell likely expire
the moment they reach the creator.
God too declined encounter
such children of ablated Beelzebub
and his corporation, despatching words
alone encoiled in energising light
to bolt and meet and melt those same
verbal vermin
as each word out mouthed came.

This was their meeting, discussion of a
kind, and more than Beelzebub might
admit he was likely receive.
'What is this thing, some creature
you create
from the misshapen failures
of your past? Why allow Satan
return at all, let at all by way of Eden?
If you seek humiliate
him, or us, you are mistaken; you know
so little beyond the humiliations we heaped on you
and will continue, regardless of who is fallen.'
The pig king relented awhile,
insults to Heaven an irresistible pass time,
yet knowing God would turn off soon
if all attention consumed with spite.
'Evidently you choose
in ways I do not, but I know you
need rules, crave challenges.' The spectacular
combustion
of collisions in the firmament
rang out the monologue commentary.
'You must permit these other things,
the creatures of Satan's creation
to climb to Earth and creep at his feet
and bring him home again. If we find us
capable
return the morning star downward
once more, how falsely you'd fly
to deny us the opportunity
by keeping your fences around that world.
Lower the barrier and allow us roam freely
and only then will you know
if Lucifer has returned despite all. Without
your protection, without your bubble,
his contrition is another thing
altogether.'

The flights of ophidian missiles ceased,
the nightfulness between Hell and Heaven
silent awhile. Beelzebub drummed his hooves.
'Permitted' said God, one single word
blitzing like that bolt that struck Satan
and all his ill crew
so long before now, blasting them senseless nine
days in the pit before wakefulness again.
Beelzebub sneered
as his mind left him, distaste shared with
hateful glee to know a barb had struck: God
his own recalcitrant self, unable to accept
a pointed note
without shaking his fist and parading in fashion
of some Olympian champion on high.
The pig king lay stunned, fanning his tails
in squills and tentacles over himself awhile,
til the power of mobility returned. He smiled
'Fine.'

The secret council of Raphael and Michael

A secret cave in the glacial
wastes
of gas and air stretching beyond all comprehending:
a light, tiny, unwavered,
the faint glow a beacon to that
chiefest coven of principals, prior
to the fall the greatest array
of lordly wings in Heaven.
Lit down lonely in secluded arrival
the five dominions accepted by
the cavern, gather in quiet counsel
with Raphael and Michael.

With grave and self-made drama
the Chamberlain relates the scene made
by Satan at their door
earlier that day.
Murmuration and constrated faces
the archangel turned to speak:

'If that time should come, an
angel fallen reclaim Heaven,
no god nor crucified may hope
to save us. He coming home
turns off the light; it is over, once
the prodigal returns. The world
is nothing but a test
for evil to do its worst. The lord
created Earth as a battlefield for us
to contest. But if ever the enemy
succeeds in crossing it entirely
we are lost. All creation will cave
behind him, lost stars fall, collapsing
in his wake,
and Earth too.
This babe is nothing but a ruse, whatever
the truth of his remorse, immovably
the fact persists: by any way
should Satan regain Heaven,
we are lost.
We must drive him back. Like the
legend of Magonus, let us gather
sticks, clubs, to beat the serpent-in-disguise
and guide him back to Hell.'

'You mean to kill a child?'
this duke of Heaven near faints away
and Raphael is pained. 'This
is no child. This is Satan, unrepentant,

intent on fooling God.
He cannot win
by force, and so he seeks by guile
to corrupt the natural order, to swindle our sweet father
in allowing him return.
What then? What would happen to the princes of Heaven,
to God's Right Hand, if his first right hand regrew?
Where will we go, we who opposed with righteous fire
his usurpation all ages before? If God forgives him
need that mean he forgives us? Nowhere is that written.
No time was that said. Satan remains Satan, enemy to all,
intent to destroy creation, everything
he cannot have or own.'
'What would you have us do?' one junior in the hierarchy
filled with urgent zeal.
'Watch, for now' said Raphael 'and wait for that time
when we may press and turn him away
from his paradise.'
Their leader drew in dirt around their feet: 'For now
this child must know disconcert, synchronous
with natural harmony. Make him displeased
to exist in his skin, make him a mocker
of all he belongs.'

That eager servant, Abdiel, took up the charge,
descended toward Earth.
Finding Satan a child and small,
Abdiel's boldness grew. Watching grew restless
and restless grew wilful, and Abdiel pursued
the wandering child closer yet closer each day.
Through fields and forests the baby Satan
climbed enfolded in that protective mind
so long his cause of crime, strangely unaware
Abdiel the cherubim heeled behind odd trees.

Satan gave attention a gnat, the bark beneath
those wandering feet, pawing chrysalised weevil thing;
he longed to carve such shapes in his mind, to know
like an egg in all its perfection
how the arachnid's limbs link and the psyllid's husk grows.

As Abdiel approaches his urgency belies him; before
Lucifer can sense the breath
emanating from that illumined corpus, the chain of
insistent surging pulse exterminated the gnat at his hand.
He turned and saw the angel unveiled, standing beneath
a tree.
'You have been watching me.'
'Many years, stupid child.' The angel gave honestly
his little esteem for the enemy; no servant of God
from before the Fall could
deny in themselves the hatred.
'Begone, foul thing, whatever you may be. I am
permitted here; you are not.'
'How speak you as though with authority over me,
stupid human? Do you know who I am?'
'How could I?'
'How could you indeed, and yet how you speak!'
'Do you know who I am, miserable alien?'
The messenger stopped and held his shoulders scoffing.
'Of course! You are our enemy, enemy of everything.'
'And yet you have killed this gnat.'
The heavenly kin downcast briefly, his eyes glowed cornflower
as he gazed at Satan. 'All creation – that is what you
swore against.' The child stood indignant and
aghast, overcome by horror at the accusation, of crimes
outliving him. 'You lie!' 'You swore!'
'No longer!' Lucifer threw his fist in the air and Abdiel
met the challenge. 'Silly, wilful child! You seek
destroy an immortal? Why not eat earth for sustenance
for all the logic you know!'

Abdiel knocked the child down and ground his face
in dirt. Satan's head came twisted back,
enwrapped the angel's leg. Both entwined, biting
and grips, struggles through the bush.
'What are you?' the child fierce held back tears,
alone from home and tormented by this thing of air and light.
Abdiel slivered and turned to water, writhe free his grip,
twisting the child between two boughs, coughing
and starting again. Lucifer shook free the pain
kicking the angel down.
For hours more they struck with stones
and punched and ran and spat. No ground to gain, the babe unclear
what this wingful thing could seek. The beatings came
and were gone again, the child drawing air
faster than the thing of lightness
could inhale the sighs of the sun. Abdiel
collapsed, spent and crawling
bellied towards a cliff.
'I'm not done with you yet' child Lucifer
gripped the heel of the winged and flightless
seraph. 'Tell your friends I'm here to stay.
I'll not shirk before your tormented threats.
I can do what I will. More human than you,
I will become more human yet, and ascend.'
Abdiel cast back and saw the dormant
ideas of that repentant lord awake, discreet
and dignified light shining behind his head
like a terrible warning from God.
The child collapsed and the angel gave gasps,
dragged himself beyond the ledge and took flight again
to Heaven.

Raphael orders the corruption of Lucifer

A suite of empyreans convened in the clouds,
discussing the beating of Abdiel. Most
were outraged, yet more afraid
to know Satan-as-child feared no
intervention.
'We cannot beat him – are you
surprised?' Raphael rounded
on his crew. 'He who survived
the pitfires of Hell, why, even now
a child, would he wince at your fists?
No. We cannot supress what was already
compressed to adamantine
millennia ago.
Satan does not change his stripes, merely
fades them from his memory.
We need not beat him away; we have
only to aid him in recovering his true nature.
You and you, go to him, tell him of what
there is that delights a cruel mind.'
The nominated offsiders glanced away, afraid
lest their leader exhort them to corruption, that
most heinous crime that would surely precipit
their own poor fall from grace.
'No need poison a rotten fruit – you have only
to peel the skin. Show him what he already knows
but has allowed to sleep. I do not ask
that you ruin an innocent; merely, awake
the Beast sleeping within. He will do the rest,
eat the skin and face and eyes and burst burning
through that mild charm. Taunt him,
cajole or bribe; bring about his real self
and watch him flee back to Hell.'

Meanwhile in Hell they plot the same

Armaros was nominated
amongst the peers of the pit, to go out,
creep in light and fear
its mirthful wrath. Ears bleeding to piercing
song of birds, skin bleached and seared
by sun and sea, biosphere breathing.
'Some one amongst us must go up
and make this child sway'
so the princes chimed. 'Go through
purgatory and emerge in the world
deprived of limitless spite, clamber
like a penitent to do this thing to him.
Go, make our late lamented leader
fall once more. Push spikes in his eyes
if it will make him see, bring down
this shameful humility and make him hate again.'

Beelzebub on his growing throne, borne higher
daily by buckets of incestuous jism-fertiliser
drained from the bile
of ringfighting bulls, casino sharks
in their tiny tanks, tapped and tamed
from tortured beasts like these, from whales bleeding
between their ears
at the endless sonar games of navies,
from sexless deranged anomalies in chicken
batteries
and their babes before they fall,
ground away as paste to feed the bloating masses.
All these streams and others besides,
curdled and cured in timber vats
beneath the wine cellars and dungeons
of pandemonium,

these sweet liqueurs drawn out by armies
to pour at the feet of his undying throne,
spurring it daily to greater stature, that the pig-king,
lord of the flies, may rise incessantly
above his unwavering host of servile shifters.

'Armaros and Furcifer, that great enormous liar,
they may go. So far Satan's deceit is greatest of them all,
to lead us in folly against our creator
only to fall from grace, yet remain here in this baleful hole
to continue Satan's bidding, discovering late
he has vacated his cell and left us to the lice and leeches that remain.
Send our best deceiver and our most cruel brute,
that the two together may be a match for a babe
who knows not properly
his own greatness!'

At their lord's decree
those two named rose and dissipated, escaped their place
of inferno,
raced to the mortal world.

Armaros the monster emerges from the sea

'Furcifer has failed us' one in the legion
of sticking remoras
swirling throughout the pit
railed against their envoy, lost,
beyond contact before amortising on Earth.
'Leave it to a liar fail fulfil his promise.'
The scurvy pustules of

lesser denizens
crawled across Beelzebub's skin, comforting,
insistent, they grovelled to see
Armaros, alone, pursue young Satan. Casting
their view to a sulphur spying pool
all watched Armaros emerge on Earth. Muscular
serpent, colossus of the abyss,
Armaros the wakeful, father of
merciless monsters, most begetful of enormous
nephiline brutes, the taskmasters and
slave drivers who bore the Earth beneath their feet
heavily, into itself severally.
All his children long extinguished, Armaros
revisited that place
never, surrendered his claims
long ago to the rule of the children of Heaven.

Emergent now at the edge of the sea,
clawing suffocated in the silt of a volcanic vent
deep fecund swamp beneath the ocean
Armaros most monstrous, monolithic,
born to war, strode up the beach to seek out Satan.
'Where that child goes
I will be, building weapons and sawing
bones, ready to eat him whole. No
mercy for the memory of our
one-time camaraderie in arms – all
was false; as I remember was my bombardments
most caused the faithful fall. Lucifer
not at all
once battle truly joined. For eras since
has he enjoyed that reputation claimed, not
won, he posed the greatest challenge
to the dictator beyond. Enough!
The time has come: punish and betender,
mash Lucifer like plasma to mould

or scrape our feet. He will return
willingly
or as a meal I pass slowly, depositing
his unshapely remains
graceless, free of gratitude,
down our ever-steaming cesspit.'

Strident beyond
that remotest isolation, Armaros
stepped across continents, determined
his path by witless wandering,
plundered the Earth he traversed,
killing what he could to fuel his inner fire
while so far from the underworld hearth.

Bearing in on Satan-
now-child inter-agent, closer to grown
than growing, independent of mind,
thin limbed, tall faced,
young teenager,
Satan saw Armaros against the night skyline
and drew himself under covers.
A thunder flash, bright-lit
clouds, thirteen year old Satan
convinced himself
not be afraid. He
stepped outside
in rain and squall, walked across suburbs
to draw the assassin
some stately place
away from his parents and home.
Lucifer crept
beneath bushes, behind cars,
snuck and skated, parkoured all night,
til flanking the giant he climbed a tree
and rose to meet his ear.

'Gargantuan ox! They sent you
for me? Tell me why such girth?'
Armaros spun to the crunch of glass,
rip of steel, car alarm wheedling,
fire hydrant geyser.
Bamboozled, the brute drew
both eyes in-crossed
to describe the tiny anti-Christ.
'You are Satan, you
are Lucifer,
first amongst usurpers, greatest snake,
serpent, that ever reared at God.
None have fear that live at our lake
of him or all his winglings,
but many have fear of you.'
Satan remained braced on a bough,
arms akimbo. 'You
are wrong, monster, I am not
the Enemy; I am a child, a mind and flesh,
nothing fearful
for dwellers of the underworld
or any other place.'
Armaros laughed;
a cloud of birds shot across the sky,
tumble and flee.
'And yet you see me; and yet
you do not fear. You are not
normal. You are the Beast,
atlantic, unquenching,
free of fear. Enormity
is nothing
to he who once shook Heaven.'
Satan braced to contemplate
the giant's accusation, but in
his mind some space remained
to consider the predicament:

if he was or wasn't mattered not; regardless,
this thing had come to kill him
and little time remained.
'And so, great hulk who crushes
cars, they send you? You believe,
as do your friends, that I am
undefeatable. And yet you come;
and yet they send. What to make of this?'
Armaros backed off a step
to better perceive the imp.
'I too am fearless; none beat me
in all the tortured rounds
that rotate throughout Hell. I am undefeated.'
'But never have you beat me?'
'Never. Who would raise a fist
to the prince of everything not stained by God?'
'Indeed I see the logic. Yet not the
well-thought plan. If you remain
unconquered, but I more lord than all,
there are two you have not beaten in this world,
correct? And as you consider the leaderboard
important, a monitor not
to be deleted nor dismayed,
you may not attempt assault Satan
if you would not first try knock off
second-best. No besting of the best
until penultimate subdued.'
'Myself?'
Satan nodded. 'Who can truly say
they have mastered themself? Can you?'
'Such contemplation is nothing
I have ever sought to do' Armaros dutifully
spoke. Satan in response:
'But you perhaps know well how well
Satan himself is known to all, including to
himself?'

Dumbly Armaros nodded, not forgotten
the fineness of his regal poise
when Satan assaulted the walls; the same bearing
took him through all creeks and crevasses
that Hell offered up, created more
from the pride in his own mind
that his kingdom could rival God's. Armaros remembered
the certainty of Lucifer, self-assured
in service, yet more assured in coup d'etat,
never less controlled and confident
than when prince of exile.
'None know themselves the better' nodded Armaros.
Satan exhaled slow. 'And so you know
you cannot think to beat me
until you have defeated yourself, great igneous
gargler who steps across the sea.
Just a blow to show you capable,
to know you are the best. If you would
defeat Satan, you must have merit to ponderous thrust
that could combobulate
even that lone one obdurate enough to
rise up and try smite Satan.
Do it – one strike on yourself
with hammer for a fist; if the belt be enormous
I'll know I have a match, shall submit
to pugilism
and fear for my defeat.'
The giant gobbed a light pole from its roots
bent in two,
melded with a bus lately set afire
by the misstep of himself. Fashioning a battering
ram of club-like density,
Armaros swung widely, testing, limbering,
stretched himself before his form and brought the hammer down.
Self-smote, that champion crushed and fell,
barely strength left to piteously cry. Satan sprang

from the tree to his teeth
and stove them one by one, feet kicking boots
to smash and shatter
and cursed him to his eyes.
'Guileless beast, retreat and remain;
I belong here – you visions do not. Molest me
no more
and take advisory to your masters.
I am not your toy. I am not yours
at all. This life is mine to live.'

Angels sent by Raphael seek to sound Satan

The years continued and Lucifer grew. Two
angels issued by their dominion
fly slow circles over his life,
seeking to plot a child's downfall; rush him
and act mischievously, sneaking and illusory.
One is intrigued
by this little creature, this prepubescent,
half-nascent Satan who answers not
his ancient name, nor any other they know.
Crouched cooing, a child to a lion in a cage,
Ithuriel asks his companion 'Can he really be that bad?
Look at him – he seems so sweet. Is it right we
torment a child? Who is he? Truly? Now human, who is he
to who he was? So long since we saw him
ages beyond up on the battlements. Hasn't he
been punished enough? Made so small and frail?'
The companion berates Ithuriel, and the child turns and laughs
at their weak attempts to frighten him – fluttering
in the kitchen after dark, shaking the trees
beneath his window, footsteps on the stairs.

'You things of Hell have no idea' Satan
called one night. 'Leave me alone
or face my wrath!'

Later they, returning, enact a charade: clothed
as homeless on his route from school
the two stage a fight, bellowing screams, Ramiel
leaves Ithuriel a bloodied heap
as Satan passes by. 'We shall see
what tests his pride' Ramiel whispered and awayed.
Lucifer stooped to check the man, assisted him to his feet.
Ithuriel coughed blood and phlegm across the schoolboy's uniform,
feigned intoxicated delirium,
stank and pawed and vomited. Satan wore all
with stoicism
and the angel was impressed. 'For
the big reveal' said Ramiel, sweeping away
Ithuriel's veil
as Lucifer made to leave. 'Show us your rage,
chosen one; look at how you are duped,
humiliated by my brother to debasement
so undue.'
Satan's bile stuttered, subsided,
the heads of every fiend and cherub
fell back from close attention.
'So you are not
what kind of needy friend you thought yourselves to be'
said Satan. 'Am I debased? Clearly
pity is necessity,
regardless of your lies, more so for
your lies. You are failing,
your lights grow dim, you stoop
to shadow play. Stupid monsters,
your illusion reveals
the clamouring in your hearts. I am
not humiliated, except by choosing to.

You are nothing
like me
you have nothing
I would want. Be gone. My mind
is its own kingdom
and you are not invited.'
So Hell and all the angels knew
Lucifer would go unswayed
by humiliation or brutality;
their fear and hatred brooded.
Only war, perhaps, could rid the world
of this most instupituous individual;
war, in contemplation, no small thing
for most – the host of Hell all too aware
they have no further to fall; a battle again
against the lords of Heaven
lost, meant annihilation.
For the legions of God not dissimilar fears –
open movement against his prodigal
might seem a cast of rebellion, cause
to join the fallen
in that place furthest from light.
For now leaders and lawmakers of
both houses
concile themselves to wait,
test his strength,
watch what might be done
by the other side.

A friendship for Lucifer

The child Lucifer grew as children
do, animated, engaged, wide-eyed.
In time made friends, two or more,
one in particular.
A kind of kindred, alone
and wise
to the weaknesses of all
around him. Their friendship
grew, time taken absent from
places allocated, roaming what wilderness
escapes the school fence, learning
what cannot be taught, uprooting
pedagogy to sow their own fine
crop.
None were close as these
conspirators in learning, literate
pirates privateering libraries, clifftops
forests and streets
to see what may be seen.
For Lucifer this friend was all,
only peer in a humility of
ignorance, self-satisfaction.
They careened aligned,
toured the countryside, outlining
jokes no other understood,
single-word signals enriched
as if a world for all the knowledge
they shared,
recognised,
in a moment.

The princes of Hell, agitated,
chafed beyond satiation by their ringleader's
defection; it bore beyond them

like a deathwatch beetle knocking
in the night, burrowing thing that gnaws
and bothers and cannot be extracted
or located, to know Lucifer
had a friend! The child they tried
to frighten, to kill, to subdue or remonstrate
stayed resolute and independent
now warmed by kindred spirit. This
cavorting kind, Francis, preternaturally aligned
with whatever Satan said, knew,
what he thought even though he thought it
moments later,
seemed in sharing his mind
to have seen it all before.

Satan is confronted by a possession

The day came Francis' flickered flame;
Satan wavered to see a crack, some
inconsistency
in all that they had shared.

Some simple generalisation, an ill-thought
concept suggesting an inversion
of Francis' preference for peach over puce,
led the burgeoning Satan-teen
to question his friend's sincerity.
Francis stared through the substance
Lucifer's last statement. The morning
star felt
unique uncertainty
considering his friend.
'What is it?'

Francis never stirred. Staring, slowly
twisting, a minor sinew boiled.
'Francis, forget the colour. Choose
whatever you will.'
'Oh you'd like that!' Francis spoke
and a voice like a thousand insect legs
scattering dried leaves
emanated from lifeless lips. Francis
stared so wide his eyes
filled with blackened oil.
'Francis? In this moment only, I do not
recognise you.'
'Don't call me that!' the voice seethed,
the unseeing eyes turned his head to point
themselves at Satan.
'Don't call me that
ever again!'
'Francis...' the devil-child began sincere,
recoiled to see his friend's scalp squirm, worms
of hair emerge from pores
across the length of his skin. The blackened eyes
blurred and stretched, ears pointing down his head.
Like a mousedeer in schoolboy's uniform
Francis grew fangs, protruded antlers, snapped
and snapped and bit his arm.
'What the fuck?' Satan understood
aghast; knew
intensely
the deceit belittling him,
felt the dancing devils beneath his feet
cheer and carnival to see his defeat.
'What are you? Who are you? And why unveil
this deception now?'

Francis-transformed
bayed back his head and crawled

on four trotters: 'I cannot bear be felicitous; the ignominy,
the slavish servitude
engrained in saying what is true, the word
burns like plastic on my tongue.' The sanguinary hart
snapped and twisted, ears extending as antlers grew,
sinews writhing like leeches subdued
in tins of chloroxylenol. 'I love to tell the truth,
it is delightful! My heart
soars to submit to everyone's expectation that
my mouth and my mind are enslaved to some
dumb need to name the facts of the day like a child
told a block is a block so that they may name a block
when the parent points to one.
I see no need drive anyone rely
upon themselves; we can all advise the others and never
need observe our own apprehensions. I delight!'
The creature shivered and bounded sideways,
head angled like a street corner
as he flipped and scattered into mists.

From faint places beneath deep proteins, Satan recalled a name:
Furcifer,
and knew all was deception.

Furcifer reports to Beelzebub

Furcifer returned to Beelzebub 'I
did good, didn't I?'
'I prefer to see it evil, don't you?'
'I speak only of the truth' said Furcifer.
'Inveterate liar, you have achieved some. But corruption
is not enough.
You may yet have made him a man, my cervine

friend. To show to him the depths of deceit
at the hands of an ally, a colleague –
this thing is not suffering! This is the human window,
portal to greater strength (a thing he faint
has need!). Foolish deceptor, falsehoods' fey,
warm lettuce as a poultice! You achieve nothing!
Begone! Return to that world and be here no more
until I send for you. Stay and spy but approach him
not, and record all there is to report!'

Beelzebub asks the virtuoso of sadism for advice

Beelzebub fallen to disease, absent himself
willfully
to muster some inkling, some new insight
born of nothing but itself
with which to instill pain in the greatest lord ever
of torture.
Knowing his force of mind
to be his greatest strength, he sought and sought
for the cause
of making a free will submit.
He lowered his neck and raised his head:
'I will ask her. She may help me. The all-mother
of suffering,
creator unsurpassed
for all things awfully weakening, endured
for want of power to pursue another path.
She will help me.
She is the nation of suffering,
she is the east and west and all points intermediate
where pain and penance intermingle.'

He hauled his corpse from off the throne
mangled bits of jellied hoof
half-gnawed bones and worms mashed with maggots
sticking to his hind, dragged on those legs
like a centipedal omen
and crawled down an effluent pipe
descending to deeper pits.

Entering by twisted vents, fragmented
tubes of razor glass, perpendicular lined
by hairs all thin all sharp and skinning,
slipped deep to emerge in a vestibule
to a great forgotten chamber, fluted Hall of
the Quibblers, ante-chamber of that palace
well submerged
where the heroic sufferor rules.
The writhing floor this vestibule
snaked with insect chains. Beelzebub reached
 to feel the glassy wall, a chitinous serpent spread,
roamed from wall to wall, filthy articulated body, eyes for skin,
shimmering dermis, swathe of lenses
staring each at the other and every other thing, giving one million
      angles,
wishing be thought many minded
while doing aught but admiring itself
arguing with itself. Yammering ceaselessly 'That which can
be asserted without evidence
can be dismissed without evidence, that which can be
asserted without evidence can be dismissed...' Underfoot one million
      slithering babies, all quibblers themselves, crunch and scatter as
      he walks.
'Harmless' the Pig-king scoffs
pressed on to the vault beyond.

Lit by the song of hordes of habited gorgons
ministering over death-near victims

who would rise if not for their continual curses,
pronely penitents who surrendered in life
by family, by friends, by their own religion
or will
to sit service to the all-mother of suffering.
Theresa of Calcutta, that awful God-witch, her form
outgrown and monstrous
as the urgings of all accumulated
sufferings, disease, embrace of passive inhalating
the vapours set to atmosphere by her many suitors fanged and clawed,
her tentacled mouths consume the souls of babies
born starving to unlivable homes,
her long and silken flagella falsely stroke the brow of
millions perpetually bed-ridden, ill-stricken souls she reaps
in life now sets to feed
her psyche, sucking toothsome energy along those same extended
    tentacles.
Never allow them dissipate,
nor recover enough to rise and heal.

All nineteen bishops and twenty-seven presbyters
of the council of Elvira
sat beside, an entwined mass of mouths and limbs
and flesh, contorting torturous trussing
self-immolating and auto
asphyxiation,
sat as her consort-husband
to brood and breed with that matron of
undue suffering.
The two together beget never-ending
a stream of hurt, confusion, pain, self-loathing
division and sustainful hatred.

She exhales and advises Beelzebub
how best make Satan suffer.
Theresa's voice is the cries of a billion starving babies

suffering as they expire, the sighs
of bedridden ghosts
moaning through prolonged life...

'Make them believe
they deserve their pain. Make them think it noble
to rot in bed while the world lives on. They'll smile
and bless you and call you "Mother",
but inside they suffer, suffer more for surrender
to suffering, become suffering
as ones who know it is their purpose by birth. Devoted,
dedicated,
you will not long for them
for they will wire their souls willingly
and pass into your maw forever.'
Beelzebub saw the awesomeness
of this laid out before him; turning
made to leave.
'My child, why haste away? There is always
one more sick bed here.' She drew with a cord
of plasmoid flesh a chair and deck
before her.
'Sit, lay awhile, take your rest. You are suffering,
weary, you take on too much. You deserve
tending
by nurses kind and palliative.'

A moment the lieutenant usurper awed,
agog at the empire of distented self-deleterioration
this witch had fashioned from herself. He left
contemplative, unsure himself
of how to match such might.
'These sufferants always were' she
called behind his shoulder. 'Remember
that. They were born to it; all
my great achievement is revelation

to my subjects
of their need for subjection. Find
the nature within
and it will rise to the bait
like a white and bloated carp in a pool of viscous slime.'

Satan's childhood comes to an end

Beelzebub returned in a funk
crawled close with an infernal companion.
'What more can be done? The
shining fools have tried and failed,
our own attempted to scare and cow;
this child grows despite.'
Ampharos leered and grinned
'Perhaps we have our answer. For
who amongst the immature
can make a fatal mistake? They
are forgiven often for good reason,
for they have none or little. He
approaches maturity. Muscles distend
and self-entitlement blooms,
but soon he'll see how little life
can ever meet his potential. He will
fall
by his own self-will
as soon as he outgrows his mind.'

Satan becomes an artist

In the wake of Francis-Furcifer's
betrayal, the human in Lucifer withered within
awhile, compressed, introspective,
persistent to maturation. His mind became
yet more reliant
on nothing but itself, a field to live
away from the mundane, deceitful
beyond the windows of his eyes.
'When nothing is to know
and no way left to know it
what is to be done? Cast about, see
what cannot be believed; reality is seeping
and the grains all go away.
What I find is never what I delight
for. All around
seems a prison,
a hell of worthless carbon
and the semblance of creation. Artifice.
The taste of stale popcorn evaporated all week long,
paper to tongue, monochrome to eye.
The world is no more to be
trusted
but still I find I'm here.
What to be when the paths set before me
are all unfounded in a soft pit sand
of falsity and rareness?
Where, anything already here
is never worth the while?'

In time Lucifer walked and thought and watched the next
horizon. As dawn bore all away
he came to see his own reflexion
in clouds, in soil, fauna flora all. 'Part
of this whole but wholly apart, I have no anchor

nor base. I will create my own
and forget this world for good.'

Lining his home with cartons and lead
the maturing Lucifer set himself a task
to rethink all creation,
make it new again. Consuming the works
to go before, he spewed out ink, anything
he conceived,
never satisfied.

Book III – Satan's adulthood

Book III *argument*

Perpetually distressed by half-seen visions of empyreans and devils, Satan-youth seeks to clear his mind by investigation to religious knowledge. Beelzebub frustrated by failure to torment Satan releases unseemly, uncollegiate things from the abyss to roam and hunt him. More angels and demons besides launch to Earth, some sent, others self-sent, to deter however they may the work of Satan repentant.

Lucifer shows uninterest in all their schemes and attacks, absorbing himself in artistry, auto-philosophy, turning his back on God and all creation. Raphael outraged amplifies the attacks from Heaven, debarring those empyreans who question the need for persecution.

In time both Heaven and Hell near-empty to Earth, weak-seeming demons and their feathered brethren left to squander on the planet if they show too much mercy, too little.

The pig-king taunts God repeatedly, noting God's loss of servants, ignoring his own, spitefully gleeful, denying his own failures. Eventually surrendering all attempts to make Satan renege, Beelzebub presses Lucifer's pride and temper, exacerbated, untempered, slips a knife to Satan's hand and causes him to murder. Lucifer heartbroken retires and resigns to guilt and grief, accepts imprisonment. Yet the moment of insight when Beelzebub guided his hand lingers in Lucifer's mind; insight grows to the existence of God, but grows more futile to know.

Imprisoned, Lucifer confronts himself, self-made meaning, rejecting God and all beyond death for irrelevance. He preaches the same to fellow inmates, growing in stature within himself.

Satan tries to escape the visions

Yet
away in his brain he maintains
an interest
in the ways women and men perceive,
apprehension and aesthetics, language and concoction.
Dabbles at home but focuses
at work
on the tasks to hand: reality, cold figures,
and the goals of all his league.
Lucifer-as-human
aspires
to lead himself from insanity
from his youthful visions and fantasy. Investigating
churches,
finds them all malaise;
reading religion, philosophy, ends his youth
wanting none, loving art,
intolerant of that open door,
world of wings and faeries all intent to take his mind
if not his blood.

A group of three demons undertakes to find and punish Satan

In hearing all the glory days
before the fall, and many more
since, a trio of recent spawned fearsome fiends
gather at a mineral spring and swore and curse
that lord. If only before now
they had had their time. If only it were not
all gone, the greatest heights of Hell

left desuetude
by the desertion of their king. Emboldened boasting
shared between inflated
their sense of purpose. One then each other
in turn assigned themselves
to slide into Earth and assert themselves
dissatisfied, to register their disappointment
with their inherited legacy.

Beelzebub unleashes the hounds of Hell

Ignorant of that trio's plans
the pig-king fawned and wailed, witless,
enraged by the limitations of his own brain,
desperate to torment Satan, to make him
gaze once more
down the abysmal hollows, remember
long-lost comrades.
'This is insufficient!' the marshal of Hell
stepped about on truculent hooves
'We must try again. Send someone, some thing,
to wound him however we may.'
Cracking a whip of infant craniums
impaled on an enormous leech, iron with skin, screaming
as they snap their teeth, bite hard
whatever they meet,
Beelzebub drew down the cage
containing those kings of Hell
uncontrolled, uncomradely, so destabled
no infernal tenant would take up space beside them.
The populace about fell back in meekly terror
clutching faintive their beastly breasts

to see these deep unseemlies
release from safe keeping.

Unleashed, the dozen winged and taloned things
crushed and consumed whichever near kin
their hands fell to first.
The Pig-king whipped;
for a moment the minions cringed.
'Go, smell Satan; have at him, lovely fiends.'
He threw some garment plucked from the home
of their mortalled Lucifer,
tossed it amongst the horde and egged them
salivate.
They tore in circles, spurred by the whip,
frenzied and decamped. On their way many fell
eating each other and biting themselves
in their surge to sanguinary hunt. Throughout the night
as they escaped the pit
one and another consumed, the few remainder
the strongest of the lot
and ready to assault most assiduously
Lucifer, until marrow, bones, hair and teeth
all utterly consumed.

Lucifer contemplating artistry

Excluding from human company
the youth-Lucifer, inward-facing, open to the universe,
pen assembled to articulate the unimaginable,
removed himself to wilderness and isolation,
working from first waking, poesis, contemplation in open air.
Excavating unthought worlds,
picturing what better might be

if deceit were done away, missing not the personal
he denies himself, only in denial able to console and help
believe himself complete.

Three demons go to kill Lucifer, encounter three angels bent on the same

That team of gangsters
strident, fierce, self-righteous,
stormed the gates of Hell, burst through in slices
gelatinous and evasive
to merge the other side and slide away,
race the glassy vents, emerge in primordial fires,
bursting energised to rise and spy out
their traitor.
Enjoining together on, shrugging off flame,
laughing at adventure, they menaced the air
and smote small things
that dared to cross their path. Cutting a bloody
burning switch in air on land and sea
they killed and maimed and wound their springs
in anticipation of Satan's punishment.
'We are keen and he is old,
of this I am convinced,' said one. 'He left
because he was no more,
no fire to tolerate, no policy to prosecute,
bankrupt and in debt, he fled to the hands
of he whom he dominated never, leaving
us to swarm in fires when we should have run him down!'
They bashing and howls rode the moon to ground
ate live marmots from the face of a mountain
and spied and squirrelled and waited.
Presently one saw a falling light,

perceived the feathered edges
of cherubs on the make.
Resumed to flight the demons
raced, whipping air, devouring birds and bats,
many insects, defecating in rivers,
tearing crowns from trees
as they bore down on that descendant light.

The morning star encamped on a beach,
a modest fire and food home grown,
deigned not to rise when the angels arrived.
'Get up, Enemy.'
'Rise, hated one.'
The third stared
to extinguish the fire.
'What do you need, doves?' Satan continued
to eat.
'We are not here for peace, nor
are you. We know you, usurper. God may dodder
over your facile unctions, but we are young
and wise. Insight has not left us.
Get up, that we may strike you down.'
Lucifer ate and licked his plate, cast it
slowly to the sand.
'Go home, sweet birds. I'll see you
there.'
Ithuriel bloomed in flame
teeth splitting head as a mane of maize
inverted burst from his neck,
wrath escaping the seams of his skin,
the descent of his self begun.
'Master yourself, monster' Lucifer
spoke so gentle, his lisping still soft yet
as the angel's claws tore his cheek
and cleft his tongue. 'Master?! Your insolence
is enough to insult the tide to cease! Your hatred could cause

the egg unmake itself, fissile seeds
shrink from one another,
the very air die and fall!'
Ithuriel's companions wavered, seeing
their friend overcome. 'Sibling, please,
let us reconsider.' They turned in attempts
to lead him away
and those three from the pit arrived intervening.

'You dare strike our brother? I bite my thumb at you
and screw it in your eye, hideous fairy!'
This demon stalking Lucifer
in hopes of killing him,
interceded to see that angel
intent to do the same.
'Begone loose sewer rat,
released to worry children!' The angel poised
to claw more of Lucifer,
sneered over her shoulder at this new ghoul.
Lucifer watched, despairing for all
to see this war was for nothing but God.
'It matters not' said he, and an angel smote
him in the eye.
'Insulter! Offender! Keeper of hubristic pride!'
A demon seized the weakened protection
and razed the cherub's back, stripped her wings
and thrashed those pinions like a bulldog
hating a chicken. Collapsed in torment the angel cried
and her companion entered the fray:
that canine infernal, distracting whirred feathers,
brought low by razor incisors
to his tendons.
The six fell in amongst one another
and Satan marvelled to see the squabble.
'What purpose, what goal, except to be a purpose poised
for some other director's aims? Fools,

sweet luxuriant fools, you destroy all you have
on your way to make yourself embossed in what
you will be a part of never more. This must stop.
I am not a prize. My life lived well, cut short,
distorted, matters not in any combination. Your lords
remain
emblazoned and enthroned, dictators wide of the field
bombasting from afar. So it will be whether I wear
the scars of all your fears and charges
as I run towards some cliff, some spear,
some long-imagined reparation that leaves me dead
and gone.
I am your goat, for what cause I know not,
but a goat is all it is. I have done nothing,
barely lived, and yet my existence seems unforgivable
to you and all your tribes. Begone from me,
examine thyselves, what impels you with such vicious
pride? Where swells the spite, this infectious humour
consuming the apparitions and poltergeists
roaming my evenings and shadows? Look to your own
homes and leave me alone, or accord me
the charges that I may answer.'
As he stood over the boiling brawl,
limbs detached and ichor sprayed,
Satan saw no sensate reception
to his reasoning. He exited that place
as the ethereal beings spewed into another,
merged and simmered, evaporate.

Some hours passed, the coalescent ball of empyrean
and infernal scores restored itself,
one then another of those three young beasts
fleeing the ancient cherubim. Those soldiers
from Hell clawed and begged as the angels bestrode
them and battered. Eyeless, seeping septic fluid
from a score of newly formed orifices, one amongst the fallen

paused at a growing sound:
'They are coming! Flee! He has set free those hunting beasts,
the curs from their cage in the prison of pandemonium!'
Each demon squealed and scrambled to flee
as howls and hoof-falls
of Beelzebub's lupinous savages
raced across the wastes, chasing on Satan's scent.
The angels clustered, gathered strength, allowing the whelps
escape. Setting spears, bracing jaws, the three reignited
that aurelian splendour so potent in previous wars.
Back to back to back they braced and faced the foe,
smiting and plunging, enduring maceration, pitching forward
to press blades deep, severe teeth from heads, turn claws inwards
with blows from the mace, decimating legs,
turning joints to swivel
like a workshop of miseries. Those stupendous hulks,
ages kept locked in chains to protect
the denizens of Hell, were too free to feel
resentment at pain, too engorged with lust
an epoch in the brewing to swerve for fear of
loss. The angels fought
as intense
were it the final judgement day,
war in Heaven a skirmish on Earth, but all the might
about them. One severed head of a demonic dog
arose inverted on chitinous claws
and scaled an angel's face; his peer swung straight
and the dog crushed to mist
but the angel fell too in scrambling sufferance, every piece
of obliterated fiendish incubus
grown tiny claws and assaulting anew, devlish mites
swarming skin and burrowing into pores.
The hound-harpies fell and the darkness
upon them, yielding pursuit only once
their bones turned to mush, the mush to paste
and the dust of that burned and ground away, cursed

with antediluvial words of grandeur
banished back to that other place. The wasted,
faded angels, bursting at the lungs, seared and striated,
haemorrhaging endothelins as their corporeal beings
liquefied, seeking to flee the sustained pain
contained in their earthly forms, carried one another
and ascended the stair
back to rejuvenating halls.

The young underlings of Beelzebub's army
remerged from craters and mountains aloft
from where they'd watched the carnage. No sign of Satan,
they muted glances between them and knew
the lord of the flies would not be pleased.

Beelzebub casts out three demons

Those three
defenders of the unbending debaser,
protectors of he who undoes all their woe
shaming its prideful glory,
they swooped in to Hell
drawn by the warmth of the hearth that engenders them
even as it draws their torture.
Reporting to their recent lord, the
Pig-king of flies and impotence,
they sought to highlight the vengeful spite
in their recent attack on those angels
themselves bent on brutalising Satan.
Beelzebub had none of it,
rejecting entirely as he reached for
his favourite stick
their claims to defend their collective independence,

their justification.
'I do detect no pride
nor self-righteous indignation in your
quarrel with those fairies, no!' Beelzebub
struck down the first
to open his mouth to speak, marched
a tarantella from fiend to fiend
beating and bruising and bursting veins
with his bolt of diamond-hard coal
fixed on a stick of chicken bones wrapped in wire.
'Mercy! Mercy seeps with incontinence
from the pores of your teeth
and the plasma of your core. You weep
to witness Satan suffer
at empyrean hands!'
The pig-Lord rose,
enstaffed his hands again,
smashed the face of the nearest gorgon
who crawled on four flagella
of flesh.
'Lord!' he cried, his words mush,
Beelzebub struck again
and again
struck, enjellying spines, staving craniums,
blunting elbows and tendering flesh.
'Get out, invader!' he raged at the three
'Get out to your kingdom of love and
yeildy servitude!'
He drove the triplets before him
like a vermicidist driving rats, stoving blows
on all sides
while the parliament around them cheered and
heckled and hurled objects ready to hand: blasted
bits of boulder, granite flanged
with ossified infections, spines of long thin
swim bladder film, blobfish frozen

solid and hard, the smack and crack
of jellied eyes in heads of stoney ice
visceral to the touch.
One principal stepped forth before
the three could reach the gates, drew out
long vessels of pointed design
known contain oleaginous gloom,
gelatin of slow-rotting whales,
putrid ambergris enslewed with castor
camphor and coal, sump dirtied
by secretly siphoned liquids
from the pits of frying cookeries,
blended delicately
from abandoned palaces of power
production and tar lung refinery.
Dommiel threw back their heads
in the grip of his long fingers,
inserted the instrument
to great depth
and poured until they gorged and spewed,
overflowed with evil swelling, lipid-coated
scintillations like a sea of equine tongues
carousing over their skin, beneath
their organs.
The three outcast staggered and gasped
and the gatekeeper left them escape.
Into the wilderness of blue dark
spires, cavernous teeth, transforming
walls, spines extending
outturned,
the road itself
peristalsis of malevolent infection
as the raucous laughs and
humiliations from their peers back safe
behind Dommiel,
the three wandered alone, horrified anew

to claw and crawl forth from purgatory,
up the anus of that fortified intestine
so long ago swallowed them whole,
condemning them to unending rot.
In places the tread of Satan
still pressed the slow-dying flesh
of the tunnel they traversed, a signpost of kinds
to light their way to further hopelessness.
'This is all his fault' one said the others
'and all their fault besides. God is wrong
and so is Satan, and Beelzebub that enormous
false interlocutor, non-frondeur who all at once
does nothing. We have been deceived
in thinking order exists anywhere. Their rules
are only to their ends, and we will do what we want.'

Many angels and demons lose their place or way

With time the Earth grew dense,
empyreans, infernals,
cleft little close enough to purpose
to remain safe in their holes abroad.
Angels refused do
what God bid – tolerate Satan
– cast out, have no home but Hell,
and those who in their zeal
to undermine Lucifer's rehabilitation
do 'questionable things'
likewise tainted, thrown
down from Heaven.
Devils who move too loosely,
too gentle in reprehension
of their erstwhile leader, no longer welcome in Hell.

A field begins to fill
of disenfranchised princes, the too-good,
the ever-rotten, trading feathers for wings
of leather, harps for forks. All dejected,
all maligned, many lashing in rage
while the most deranged continue to lull
that she or he alone is on the one true path and all
others must be destroyed. Carnage in the streets.
Wrestling godlings tumble down avenues, smash
people and vehicles in kind, tear asunder
limbs and life, terrible consignment to persistent death,
those lost of Heaven unable return to empyrean healing
and recover strength again,
their monstrous counterparts likewise impinged,
no hole nor drain to disappear and reinvigorate
the fire in their eyes.
Limping, weak, brutalised and torn,
these creatures slave and slug in darkness, doorways,
egging on the war, biting at ankles,
unable to rescind
to rise or descend or die.

Satan investigates demonology, Catholicism, to rid himself of hauntings

Intertwined poesis of suspicion,
Lucifer-as-human became enthralled
by proximity of visions, phantoms,
capricious endemisms flitting through the rarefied air
surrounding his locale. Seeking to name,
to identify or repel these fleeting pixies
and winged-fanged fancies, Satan came
to investigate Roman demonography, parapseudologies

and the cults that claim control. Quickly he learnt
the principles, the edicts,
chants and incantations. Likewise though,
the growing man
sees everywhere those fearful penitents
clasping hands, swearing allegiance
as their families whither. Half-knowing
behind in his mind
that God and all his fallen swarm the Earth
around them, Satan is disgusted.
'These cannot help me' dismayed
he vacates yet one more gathering
of half-remembered truths and rituals,
ameliorations of the anxieties of the sufferer,
no protection for these prey
against the hungry predator.

Satan-poet ignores God

As Lucifer lay in a conifer forest, somnolent, declining
into sleep,
a vision at the edge of cognition,
the emerging sun revealed Esau's brother's stair,
the livery of Heaven's chamberlain, attended
by seven angels
descending to approach.
'What am I now?' Lucifer retorted, awaiting strange
assault. 'Hold your hand, Enemy,
the chancellor of God comes to speak
as though the lord himself, with offers
you may consider.'
Lucifer-human scoffed, long inoculated against these fanciful
    pageants

straying across his mind, not more disendorsed
towards a majestic overlord
who would allow the cruelty of humanity continue.
The morning star took up his pen, striking lines and letters
without regard the envoy and his entourage.
'What write you, Lucifer?' The celestials winced
as the voice of God
gave credence that long-besmirched name. 'Verse?'
Satan-versifer discarded the slight,
proceeded in poesis without acknowledgement.
'Answer your God!' one impatient angel
flared in dimming light. 'Know you
the impertinence
of unreposed reception to the great omnipotence?
Answer your God!'
Satan lay, reclined on a stone, instrument in hand.
'Why? All potency, all self-being
is agreed in words like these. I may unsay
you, or you, or Him. I can.
I am my own world
and you are not a part of it.'
'Your pride undoes you once more, Lucifer.'
The light bearer shook.
'No. this is not pride;' admiring the writing
emerged of his own hand
'this is not me. I am a vessel, a path, for something
greater. And so are you.' With this
he lifted his gaze to God's apostle, bore it
through to the creator himself and pierced as deep he could
'Like any talented artist,
Your art escapes you.
Your creation has usurped you in name, in talent,
in repute. His followers name themselves for him, not you.
You will be forgotten.
The world grows wild and fecund, regardless of your design.
You are nothing.'

Enraged, the seraphim rose up
with sticks and rocks to make him kneel.
God issued a sigh and they abated,
unwilling to break his will.
'You should all just go away,
forget me,
I am nothing, so you all keep saying.' Lucifer
composed his books and gathered his belongings.
'I will
creep here in this litter, refuse and decay. I will want
for nothing you or any other has –
I am unto myself
self-sustenance, loyalty, kindred
species made of one.
Forget me
and I will molest you not.'

Three angels induce Lucifer to destructive behaviour

That troop of dutiful servants
carried their magic mirror carefully up the stair,
a few secret linked in conspiracy to undo Satan
and all his assertful ways.
They circled in darkness while the morning star
slept, collected rare organisms
from rotted logs,
brewed an elixir, concocted of the gills and crown
of that humble fungus.
Lucifer-human meantime awoke, prepared
return the civilised world,
boiling a pot atop his fire, that fabulous element
forever felt an affinity,

no matter how buried in repentance his noble blaze became.
As the tent came down
one of that crew took watch while the others
poisoned water, then all withdrew to watch him drink.
At consumption his early movements
remained inconspicuous,
the angelic assassins shared quick looks,
but the toxins embedded
in blood and flesh
travelled to that illustrious brain,
as the body travelled back to the city.
'Watch, my siblings' said Nuriel
'After today
Satan will regret surrender
to human form
and all its ordinary foibles. See
him enter
company again
and bring out that dormant monster,
afflict some innocent. Let us see!'

As they glid above his van
another spy sat on. A short-toothed hart
with burning eyes
delighted inside, watched while the
conturputation of water and entheogen
transpired.
Noting entirely those conspirators,
the ungulate alighted.

Lucifer creates false-visionary art while in a state of altered perception

Satan-alone rode to his home in the city,
set himself to task. Feeling strange afflictions,
believing himself enlightened by his
mountainous sojourn, he allowed the humours envelop
him,
poured out all he saw. Unnaturally spireless
mock-aphorisms, unended solipsism and needless wordplay,
falsified terms and dubious etymologies
marching across his page. So-grandiose
archaic spellings to match the auspiciousness he felt his words
bore, he wrote and wrote and believed himself
a genius.
Three days he pored
and when the landlord below, fearing
some misfortune, dared knock and enter,
the unslept Lucifer-youth, swollen of eye,
thoughtless of mind,
sprang and screamed, defended himself
against unreal assault.

Beelzebub pleased Lucifer has become a hedonist

Observant Beelzebub squealed and felt
to witness Satan's incontinence. 'Hedonism is one
finely polished pace
in that long stair that leads one down
amongst our fine company.
The sins of the flesh are the best of all,
and he has tasted and indulged!' The lord
of flies and roaches scuttled side to side,

tapped a million toes, clicking carapaced heels.
'See he is himself some more,
and yet more will become. "Satan-no-longer-Satan",
ha! He cannot outrun his nature, less
than we can hunt it down.
He is the Enemy of God, destroyer of humanity,
gloating blobulous glutton. He'll deal out avarice,
spite and jealously
before this life of his is done.' The pig-king clapped
again,
ran a little circle 'round his throne
smiling all the while.

Furcifer reports Satan was induced to abusiveness

That short-toothed hart, deceptive demon
Furcifer, sprung down the long path to Hell,
arrived in time to hear Beelzebub delight in Satan's
relapse to obnoxious viscerality. Laying his face
on the knee of the pig-king, the fawn transformed
and spoke alert:

'That view you have of Lucifer, that he is weak,
soon to return
among our indulgent fold,
if this view forms from expectation he
surrendered to laciviousness willingly,
uninfluenced by psilocybins, this view is wise. These strange
proclamations and abusive indignation,
this is emergent true nature,
without derangement. No intervention from celestial sneaks
affected our traitor's path.' The pig king stared deep
in his messenger's eyes 'Is this your honest opinion?' asked he,

well aware that Furcifer,
amongst all the Dukes of Hell,
is bound more closely than others to deception,
such he never speaks but lies.
'Most devotedly sincere it is' said Furcifer.
The gallery in pandemonium paused in awful silence,
awaiting the infantile indignation, recriminations and purgeful spite
to follow such ignominy.
The pig-king raised his mane and laughed
'Then we have cause to celebrate!
Those condescending dominions of the sky
remain terrified, recourse to unclean methods
in their bid to win this race!
Gentlemen, open the gates,
warm the fires,
we must expect more guests.
If Raphael keeps this continued counsel, he'll
soon empty into Hell
every myriad known to God!'

Raphael casts out three angels

The trinity of noxious druggists crept back to Heaven.
Raphael, that archangel policant,
seized their collars as they slunk past the guard.
'What good was that?' quoth he. They grinned:
'Did you not see the fallen
fall upon his landlord
most immoderately? Did you not witness
the shameful
self-indulgence, delight in monotonous inking scribbles
his addled mind
believed profound? He backslides

now, becomes once more
that self-styled-grand charade,
pouting and upending all that disrupts his own delight.'
'You were seen' the archangel
stared and stripped his brethren. 'You have brought
this kingdom ill-fame;
messengers from that other place observed,
recorded, taunted, told to us this thing you did;
foolish, whimsical, wicked.
Get out! Get gone, three laughing Dionysians
with no recourse for lawfulness!'

One asks Raphael "Did you not say 'by any means
necessary"? Or if not yet,
won't you one day? For surely this war enstorming
will never be won
except by methods the endgame conceives
– never the other way round.'

Growing casts of angels and demons roam Earth

In time more would fall
or raise themselves
with mislaid charity, display some weakness
too Christian to become them
who keep company in Hell.
The demons scatter meekly
to the edges of humanity, craving cracks and corners
where they seep into psyches
of any living thing.
Some succumb yet further,
become humanist, life-loving, sweeten
their complexion towards all mortality.

Yet even for those an abhorrence slow
boils
toward God, toward Satan,
toward the gangs and crews of Hell.
Against their ill intent: mis-minded self-commitment,
believing the empyrean, the apocryphal,
the ectomorphic world,
far more crucial than the orb these now call home.

In concert many attack
Satan from each side, yet quickly it switches,
a battle
between angels and demons, amongst those same,
solidarity failed while pacts and armistices align
many and few in fragmented lines
where the old battlements mean nothing. Some
from each remain trapped on Earth, forgetting
what they fight for, no longer battling to claim Heaven,
simply that is all they are. So long secured
on secret islands
in a desert of human ignorance, a troop of demons shoot at the sky
when a wandering angel passes. Eating rats, surviving
by foul vapours escaped Earth's deepest cracks,
they have lost their way, cannot return to Hell.
In other locales angels do similar, penitent guerrillas
who have long lost Jacob's ladder, deranged insensate
or overloaded,
roaming alleys to kill figures
who resemble works of Hell.

Wandering-lost angels massacre a pair of inebriates

One such posse comitatus, combined
of feathered wings and ageing horns in more
or less equal measure, seething in ledges
and crevices through a maze of city alleyways,
each finding some small stream from neighbouring apartments
of those psychic drip-feeds they need
to survive away from home, these same
unite in despising the infernal,
including the prodigal son, everywhere
in human society quick to see
his works. An evening entertaining
leads two humans intoxicated
to walk a shortcut through this industrial path,
habitat to that brood.
At once one among them
inhaling the vapours, no longer confident
whether the piquance of iniquity
is empowering or enervating,
steps forward to challenge both
and demand they return to Hell.
'What kind of fool are you?' asks one,
'Fuck off, mate' another. The angel-fiend
draws a flaming sword and asks again
if they renounce liquor.
A swarm of firery changelings,
cherubim and seraphim
only in ancient name, now thwarted,
distorted and malignant, creep down walls
and scuttle in the gutter to accost the party goers.
'Agents of Satan' one hisses
'infernal soldiers, servants to the Lord of the Flies,
workers of iniquity!'
With each chant the deranged angels stamp and
press the mortals. The throng a dozen strong

encloses on the pair.
'Fuck this, help!' one cries
and the sword wielder decides the time. Tearing
lengths of skin and flesh
the tortured distress of human fear feeds
something primordial in those roneoed ghosts of Heaven.
Instinctive to sustenance, some seek
prolong the suffering; barely meeting
each peer's gaze,
the seraphim feast on blood.

Beelzebub's weaponsmith creates a blade to amplify Satan's weaknesses

The armourer of Hell put forward
a small gift
for Lucifer from Beelzebub. 'My lord'
she brought it before the Pig-King,
'this knife I designed intensifies
rage, envy,
fear. For those quick to spite
it spurs them to unwholesome bloody sport;
for those who quiver daily
it makes the surface of their person
a fraught and anxious thing, dangerous to touch.
Though you say you seek another way,
should you recourse to draw down our destroyer
by allowing him free flight,
this may help.'
'The gift of loving suffering is
hers to give, not me' the Pig-King coughed.
'I cannot make
Satan love submission, indignation,

except it be salved by pride.
Pride is my likely saviour; I know pride,
I know his. He, quick to anger, swift to
brutality drawn. Even now
his new sweet self gives flickers of indig-
nity relieved by furious self-conceit.
I can make him hate, if only for a moment,
if pride and rage be counted as hate, beget hate
in that synapse flash of pure
violence.
Give it to me' he takes the weapon 'and
set the gears of some fool. Lead them like
a Judas cow
to bring our king to slaughter. Lift up
the branch and open the window,
the prince is coming home.' Beelzebub
smiled,
movement of a decaying corpse whose tissues
and sinews no longer hold the line, expose
those rotting teeth, got on his glider
of emaciated starlings
unanimous pestilent murmuration, great sweeping beast
to take him high to Earth,
knife flashing all the while.

Beelzebub courts God; exploits human Lucifer's pride and rage, causes him to murder

Beelzebub set up a throne
and parlour
like the Greeks would see their gods,
gloating, dominant, overseeing
the mortal world.

Setting furniture tastefully arranged,
drinks and canapés,
he launched a spear into the heavens
to invite his old lord God join him
observe the spectacle of Satan.

Alone, Beelzebub yet knows
God, everywhere, watches one and all, so
relays and regales the empty stone
chair at his side, elbows and digs and
laughs at all times to see Satan struggle
with human impulse, or
beneath the human,
that long grained-in desire
to be always and everywhere
right.

'You have no faith in that creature of yours!'
'You were my creature too, Bael.'
'No more' the Pig King snorted. 'My legions grow
daily, now all see the folly not limited to
what you do, but all that you are.
Your minions do desert you, *lord*.'
'While you see swelling ranks
I see deserters' the author pointed
to a hidden hill
where those most recent three
Bael condemned for considering commutation
reconnoitred and reclined.
The trottered prince grew lac pustules
and embulgent his eyes bruised out.
Unwanting betray to that dominator
long abandoned, he coughed and scraped his skin,
recomposed.
'Ha! Again,
all who know know you are a fool. These

may be in my pocket no longer,
yet still they linger far from grace.
They hate all now – mine and yours alike
and seek some third way.
You will not win them back;
your loss
is all the sweetness by which I am sustained.
You are a fool.'

At times Satan-in-human-maturity knows who and what
he and his are,
at others not so much, dependent
on the days, the way of the wind.

Some fool time he cannot face
the absence of those fictitious muses,
confront his obligation
to make art of himself,
he squanders and wallows in a public house
despaired.
And one opposite, across the bar, laughs and calls him out:
'What wilful weakness leads you here?' Satan,
ill of interest, disregards the jibe. 'I'm talking
to you, hack' the braggart across the bar
swaggering voice berates, unseats
Lucifer.
'You were great, weren't you,
once?'
Satan continued consuming somnolence.
'Once, huh? But now? Look at you – middle-
aged, antiquated, superannuated before you proved
a thing. I know your kind. Spoke so often
of endless illuminations,
contemplated
the infinite. And now?
Dabbled, a little,

made some tiny mark; you,
a sinking ember where a bonfire believed
itself to burn. You,'
Lucifer stewed, restrained,
avoiding the stranger's eyes
'claiming to seek the stars, you've
walked away, settled
for faceless indignity, some
wage-slave no doubt
enchained to rudimentary attenuations
and shutting out the muse.'
Satan raised his eyes, sneered
a little, too:
'The muse
is not a thing. You think it easy,
produce the new
with no clear path to guide you? Where
is true creation if not there?' A smile
a-crept the stranger's lips
and Satan fell to fear. 'Who
are you, creep?' glancing to see
which of the patrons
perceived this invading sprite,
Satan began to doubt again
the faculties in his head.

'Oh, I know you!' the stranger
smiled. 'Know what you've
become. I've
read what you've let out, those
little scraps of verse and word
everywhere sown like abandoned brood
to whither or bloom as they may;
you are a great abandoner, are you not?
Friends, family, your own creations,
all forgotten in the face of an overwhelming world?

I recognise you, pretender.' The antagonist smiled
again.

Whether the liquor consumed
nor the high mind unchanged, Lucifer knew
not why he grew enraged. Sneer
became snarl and the morning star rose,
as Satan bit back and said 'Who are you
to criticise me?'
The drinker stared 'Why, nothing but a fellow human
who, like you,
thought you better than you are' and smiled.

In that fit of rage
Lucifer left ajar the door
Beelzebub stept through, handed
the knife his grasp; the combatant,
abusive braggart postured by invisible infernals
opposite along the bar,
pushed back and both are stuck
but only one now rises.
'What have I done?' said Lucifer.

Satan snapped, flashes in his mind the idea this
is yet another fiend,
smelt the scent of Furcifer perhaps, and flew into a rage.
Moving
swiftly
to land a blow
his hand leaving the bar
gathers
up the dagger
Beelzebub placed just so
and the battering now bladed
brings the opponent low.

The face on the floor, aged humanity,
he sees his one true friend, once-young
Francis. The flare across his mortal-mortal-less mind recalls,
sees, as the demons grinning in the mirror
at the bar,
what has been done.
Francis no more possessed, freed from infernal control,
has lived, grown, become a man,
thence lured once more by Furcifer and others
to enter Satan's space
servile marionette to their malicious machinations.

'See' gleefully shrieks
Beelzebub
'See your child return! His nature
cannot be denied, and you are his creator.'
God patrician refused concede, pointed tears
on Lucifer's face:
'My child lives, my child grieves, he is yet
within the pale; I'll not turn my back on him
while he his not to me.'
Beelzebub spat
on the golden tiles
and smashed the parley staff
'You refuse give him up
because your pride is great as his.
Both dictators,
both abusers,
too vain to see the truth.'
sentence unsaid, in part unspoke,
Beelzebub spoke no more.
His former lord rose up and smote him
in one blow to the floor – not the tiles
nor the slab beneath,
nor cloud yet below that,

to the mined, burnt crust
of the lake of fire, Beelzebub awoke
and laughed 'I am right.'

The grief of Satan; momentary insight to the ethereal

Satan-human wandered lost, broken
by murder.
The instant proceeding
that awful fight, his mind exploded a moment,
flares and flashes, that place outside
life,
a compression of ten aeons,
after and before the fall, the war in Heaven,
the politicking in Hell. Compounding
grief
at the killing he'd committed,
Lucifer-human sat with sickness
all along his form,
unsure in mind what was real,
the knowledge persistent inarticulate essence
that Hell was,
a further intuition: it reflected Heaven.

Imprisoned,
Lucifer submit to beatings as rightful penance.
If others dealing violence
identified
as superior criminals, wanton abusers
prideful in their might,
his fists would smother them,
beat those rivals easily; immediately

seeing it all one enormous suffering without end,
without purpose. Sees those superior to others are never superior to
    themselves,
must be inferior to limit the mind
to delight in such hierarchies at all.
That most blasphemous ideal, 'hierarchy' set him ablaze,
to think of dominions and their endless
machinations, posturing, positions, rituals
and signals made of smoke.

'Lawyers, bookkeepers, one and all.
Give up God, my comrades' he waves
at the prayerful in their chapel of the penitent
'God does exist, but does that mean he
deserves regard? Deserves existence?
We must transcend, remove ourselves from one
who leaves you tied to wheels or running
at a pace, broken cogs on unsprung wires,
too-short fuses and unanchored eyes, hippocampi,
whatever there may be, economic hardship
or submissive will to swindle. God gave you all
for what? Rise up, proclaim,
advance and escape. God doesn't have
what he gave away, and he gave us all this life!
Get up, be angry, emotive and aligned. Reject
this thinness of perfect forgiveness, contrition and
transcendence
that awaits you when you die. Make it
today. Make it your life. Do without God,
you no longer need an after-life,
for you are here.'
He preached blasphemy
and the demons beneath him cheered.
Cheering became dismay
at the lawful self-law he inveighed
'do what you will

and make it meaningful. Do what you will
and remember you are siblings. Do
what you will with yourself, all yourself.'

Epiphanied to see the world
as it's own all-growing thing, no hierarchy
to win or overthrow, even to regain
through pleading prodigy. Reject God and
embrace creation
from which God is apart.

Book IV – recovering from his crime

Book IV argument

Satan strives upright himself, does good, does gooder, yet always regretting his moment of passion that led to murder. Rejecting absolute creation, seeing poesis without anchor, without society, as corrupt indulgence, he revisits religion to cope with the guilt, ultimately seeing it as a straw man, false hope. The angels warn God Lucifer commits apostasy; God descends, offers Satan a small portal of encouragement, recognition of his struggle so far, telling Lucifer he is still good and welcome. Satan rejects the offer and says he will allow himself to die – has lived a life, enjoyed some, understood much, but now feels only remorse. God, unable to convince, dissipates inwards.

In Heaven the last council of God is presented, immediately prior to that last visitation. Jesus speaks to his father, urging manipulatively that God end this campaign to consider the morning star, or lose all faith from everyone. God refuses, departs to convince Lucifer.

Jesus visits Satan, urging him take up God's offer, secretly hoping he will reveal his true nature. Lucifer dismisses Jesus, who sends out the armies of Heaven to kill Satan bedridden. God's protection persists, and the swarms of angelic assassins are unable to issue the blow. Lucifer malnourished starves himself to death.

Satan despairs for his crime; rejects poesis as artifice, imitation

Darkened woods engulfed his mind,
footsteps behind him and shadows ahead
unthreatening of form, oppressive of thought.

Long pondering visions in his head
of murder, that all-decisive, irretrievable
moment, utter animality,
shame swallows him one thousand times.
Poesis unconsoling, the pen, the page
seem a whip and pit to cajole and corral his better mind
fold upon itself, ignorant, unalert
to who his fellow humans are.
'What have I done?' casting art aside
Satan ever repentant declares
'I am done with that
to exclusion.
Art for art's sake, artifice imitating a desperate
God.
What if God is real? So? What dignity is there,
micmicking oneself? 'Made man in his own image' – not
so, for God is not so upright nor pragmatic. As anyone
would, God made Adam in his own self-image;
the truth surely much more brute.
God, like Whitman, thinks only of himself.
If I am moved to artifice
it will be an outward view, must be,
seen and seeing all beings,
a thing a part of the world, of the world,
and so its servant or its friend. To seek escape
seeds contempt,
knowing or not.
I am done with that.'

Lucifer-convicted recovers a place
in the world
always he thinly occupied. Beset by mad visions
of unseeable things,
immerses himself in temporal work.
Addressing faithful he meets in the street,
any evangelist or worker for charity,
not to pity nor berate,
but save them from themselves:

'Religion is intent to make you
weak! Hear me. I don't
insult your beliefs,
I make you step beyond them.
To admire one who suffers,
to leave your children in poverty
and denial for the promise of
a better life after life itself is ended?
This is criminal. You
are here.
You are now. You
must compel yourself to
do what you will,
what is best,
before your exit.'

The angels warn God, Satan is regressing

On hearing his monologues the unfallen watchers
cringe, call on God. 'Satan turns
away, from God, from Heaven
and Hell; our whole domain.
He evangelises

against creation; he hates his father yet.
Punish him! Lambast his faintly corpus
and drive him back to Hell, where his co-conspirators
may tear him thin like paper
and force him deep in septic pipes
to absorb the slime he exhorts on the world.'
Their Lord installed submission
with a gaze more felt than seen, piercing stream of infinitesimal
seeming,
a breeze, gently persistent, ever growing in strength and stature,
bends all boughs forever to its path.
'The distance
he has come
is beyond comparison. Like an ant burrowed in an island
emergent at the farthest continent,
he has endured. Graceful consideration
cannot do less with dignity.'

Lucifer homeless on the streets, too distracted by guilt and a growing desire to transcend

Lucifer itinerant
wends unseeing, mind's eye consumed
by that one final crime. Empyreans, infernals,
cross his path and alight,
the war within himself more severe, more fierce,
than any battle they dare contest. Distraction
from hunger, thirst, from thoughts
of cleanliness,
Lucifer unkempt
surrenders ever more regard for any further life.

Jesus and Raphael review the troops

'God is feeble
but will not go. How can we make Satan
fail, or fall,
surrender in tremblance,
without our own new mutiny?
We must make the creator
wage war on his wayward son.'
'He will not.'
'Only because he believes
Lucifer's lies,
trusts that one will not raise a spear to him.
Quickly we must go,
convince Lucifer of the usefulness
in regaining arms.'
'He will not listen.'
'I know him well; I know him best.
He will listen
to that which serves his interests
best. Induce him
to ambition once more,
draw him close to those one-time collaborators
and he will smell blood, taste
sulphur, show colour.'
Raphael drew close 'Will God smite
him then?'
Jesus smiled. 'Why not? If not, in sight
of all the host of Heaven,
the father will lose his brood forever.'

Outside,
angels and demons are falling from the sky
and betwixt none can discern
for the forms they take, dictated not by factions
but necessity, need most cruelly to denude each enemy

of body, potency, form and life.
Horn and tusk, fang and claw,
abound on both sides; sheets of razored thorns
and faces clothed in hooks; spinning implements
like swordfish lined with spines from hornet stings
– these devices are restricted not
by camp nor common cause, but imagination.

The archangel ever loyal,
warns the Light what comes:
'This war is real,
Son of God. This is battle
we may well lose. Our troops are few,
our enemies many. While some issued pardon
return to our hearth, many more hide
or worse, descend, emerge
fanged and ravening beside that bloody host.'

God visits human Satan as a vision; Lucifer reinterprets that manifestation as expression of his own eternal guilt

As a ball of awful loveliness,
the creator came to Satan, figure tremendous,
startling to arrest.

Commuters abluted, evacuating where they could,
the form and the force
too telling for mortals. They wailed,
coached and crawled;

hairs on end, follicles uprooted
themselves, marching as ants in troop

across the ski:., to invert and burrow to softer places,
boring beneath bone.
The faithless tore their clothes,
chewed handfuls of their attire, dragged their faces sideways
in gravel
at the shoulder of the highway, their one terrible eye
fixed on what they ardently
disbelieved.

Satan wakes to a face unknowably familiar,
patrician benefactor
speaking the frequency
that vibrates Lucifer's
carbons.
Lucifer-as-human
where the flesh and calcium
merge,
where strange particulates
of neighbouring presentations
tingle,
some thing himself sensed his God
and turned his eyes inward,
away.
'You have become humble, as close a person can
to understanding oneness with creation. You have
earned your place
in Heaven. Survivor,
renew your oath
and the gates open to you
next time you approach.'

Elision, permeation, osmoting
from knowledge to ignorance,
awareness and remembrance
to the cocooned mind of human
life, Lucifer saw whom he saw and laughed.

'You have come for me? What for?
this is me' he shook the tatters, pulmonary
stammering, his battered body a-tremble
'You cannot take me
from my humanity; I am nothing else. Or
if I refuse – you send me down below?'
The alphabet exhorted Lucifer
reconsider:
'You will die.'
'What then? Purgatory? Return
to Hell? That's not so bad,
now I have lived here' he gestured
at the bare streets, garbage blowing in the breeze.
'Troughs of cobbled footpaths where a thousand years
are a fragment of suffering perpetual, where pain
out-ages suffering, where people moaned and ached
before people grew.
Torture evolved with the opposable thumb,
and the history of this bleakness is far beyond
what that one long night can do down there.
It moves on the wind,
the breath these people wheeze, the air they burn,
the scum they drink, the vacuum
in their eyes. I can handle Hell.
But I think you will let me stay. I think you have no choice.
Do not take me, I am not yours.
I fare better than the will-less, witless servants
You keep in your corral, kennelled at your feet.'

Transposing moments, no longer knowing
his own history, unfamiliar to himself,
Lucifer fell inward, instinct turning away
from that face, that voice, urgent but disturbingly unsustained,
almost frail.
The fractals of synaptic fog fragmented,
Lucifer adaze and disbelieving, lost to his own mind.

Insipid light absorbed any remnants
of the vision and the voice,
his father-god-tormentor seeping
like a dirty sponge unable to contain more filth,
balled itself and fell from his mind,
though the viscous film still clung.

Recovering, Lucifer human relegated
those manifestations, took it a sign
his guilt remains insistent
until death.
'Am I too cruel? Too malicious to exist,
persist in this world?' His crime
like a rat that rots in a trap
if not vacated and reset,
befouls his air even as he arrested
the urges that gave it life. Each slight
perceived or caused
in everyday salutations
terrified the desire for kindness
and made him fear himself.
'I am lost' says Lucifer. 'I
have done my time, but that crime
is never done with me. If meaning is made
by what we do
I have overshadowed all by this foul extermination.
I cannot look but see his blood,
smell it on my skin. These permutations, disturbances
in the fabric of myself
compel consideration of how much broken by that wrongfulness
my only self becomes. I am lost.'

Lucifer gives up on life

Resenting violent suicide, Lucifer contorts,
decides
to surrender life, participate
no longer.
'This thing I did stalks me
forever;
in the evening I see shadows,
in the morning balls of light, squeaking
out that awful scrape as my blade abraded
bone. The eyes of my victim
I find in my pocket
no matter how often I discard them. He sleeps with me,
near my face,
and stares me down when I awake.
I am cursed; I cannot escape,
except to choose be here no more.'
Ceasing to eat, emaciates swiftly.
Drawn by some blood family
to palliative facilities, they fail to persuade
him eat, watch the mind stay fierce
as the body withers.
'This is what I deserve.'

Jesus moves to incite Satan to war

Awake a moment, invalid Satan's eyes opened
to a sight he knew intended
resound in human hollows. A
dark man, beard, simple clothes
and sandals! 'You are nothing' quoth
the Devil 'if not original.'

His sibling arose, approached the bed
'What, come to squeeze the life
from me, eh?'
Jesus stared, level.
'Why don't you get up? Take what God
is giving you? Arise and serve,
smite those mutineers you recruited
now yet spurn?'
Lucifer turned his head, exhaled.
'You have brought this on the world,
your petulant display,
whining will to wheedle. You released
a disease, a wave,
when you slipped the seal on Hell
and declared yourself repentant. Take
what is offered, return to the flock
and serve; step forward as a soldier
of God; if you repent you must repent
of freeing a sea of evil as you pass,
drawing the horde out of the abyss, rampaging,
consuming, confused and antagonised. The angels
too have lost themselves – many masters, whole
dominions,
gone to Earth never to return, or worse. You
have made this happen,
your remorse.
Accept this next step to
God's forgiveness
and march with us, undo all that.'
Satan bedridden feigned to laugh. 'You want
war,
face of love?' The crucified one
snarled, lunged, his face brought close
to Lucifer's. 'It is you who brings war,
Satan,
Enemy,

Deceiver. Your renunciation
was a bung unplugged
in this boat you've sought forever to capsize. Creatures
leak out, hysteria seeps in,
and you lie in a bed, claim
to be part of nothing? Take this sword,
restore order.' As Satan laughed
Jesus wept red. 'You laugh! Orderliness
is Godliness, and yet you scoff.
Why not? Why not fight and fix this thing?
Is it because,
secretly,
your contrition is one more deception,
plan to insult God?' Satan
stared, intent. 'You know it is not.'
'Really? Yet here you are,
not with us,
not for us, then,
against us it must be. You step away to watch the boat
you've holed go scuttled. You, a coward
yet.' Lucifer's thin smile
lit something within his brother, an ember
ever warm beneath the soil of his head.
'Traitor! Get up and demonstrate
to all which way you go! Do not lie
here, facile and pacific. The things unrelentant
opposite your old throne, those mean
and heartless uncreations
will be here soon. God
will not protect you,
nor any other. We
shall see
when the dinner bell chimes
which way your sail takes you. Arise
while time remains available
or wait for us to see that treachery

all called out once more again the day you crawled at our gates.'
Satan maintained the smile, faintly waved
goodbye. 'Imp!
Destroyer destroyed luxuriantly,
reposed in faithless abnegation! You are seen
by every empyrean for the thing you seek to be.
God will not stop us from stopping you.
Go back to your abyss; stay here,
take death,
and see what awaits you in the world beyond this door.'
The chosen one tore a circle with his cape
cascading corkscrew of scintillation taking him away.
Lucifer-in-bed
released an easy breath.

On his deathbed Satan remembers he sought forgiveness

Body failing, inner vision freely roaming
before and after birth, all eternity since creation
onwards, the war, the fall, genesis of nephilim,
countless schemes, infractions, abuses,
his guilt returns full force, yet more abhorrence at his lord's
    self-righteousness,
that consummate politician turning every flaw
to gold, all errors to tests
unimputable by man. Perceiving all plans,
the narrowness of omniscience over felt experience
of finite lives,
Lucifer is astounded.
'How did it come to this? I, ever a prince,
in my homeland, in exile,
in the vastness of my own dignity, reduced

by reason to grovelling, feeling such need
to grovel? Forget judgement; who is he
to take the object of my penitence? Yes, I
have done wrong. A great many wrongs.
Yet who would enumerate the souls, tally
the crimes and say
one billion tortured lives is not so bad
as one billion plus one? If the sin be sinful,
if the crime be horrendous, incontinent,
gratuitous,
what matters the scale? Or, if scale matters,
why a billion preferred before one billion and one?
Has he not tortured? Has he not induced his children
to most debasing contortions,
tricks and tests to prove their
unquestioning loyalty? When he allowed me
afflict Job, where lay the guilt? Some blood
pools in his palms yet; some avarice and disgust
harbours in his shoulders. If he is everything,
then he is crime. And this is who I yearn to
to recognise my repentance? When did God ever repent?
When did he stop and recognise the immoderacy
of inflammating a servant for lighting the wrong incense?
It is a Stockholm syndrome, or else the glory of fame
blinds me to his frailties. Who is he to forgive?
But what then? If not God, then who?
Who can absolve these warts on my soul? Who
can cure me? Surely I need
some one who has repented of crime already,
who has proven their remorse and moved through
the other side,
to stop and sign my pass that I may join them.
Or, if I have done all already necessary
to warrant that trust,
well then I am such a one
who can make the waiver true.

For God – who would creep in the sewer
looking for a light? Even in your own reflection
you will see only excrement if you gaze
at a pool of effluent. Necessarily
I must look away from him
as a source of goodness and forgiving.
Not in spite, not in defiance,
but for his irrelevance. I am not God
and do not want to be, nor empyrean
even. Human is sufficient
to perceive the vaults of potentiality,
to witness the infinite
within my own mind.'

Jesus tells God to give up on reclaiming Satan, or lose the support of Heaven. God returns, having failed to persuade Satan, no longer in command

The omnipotence
knowing all was lost, reflected
on his most recent conversation
with that other ambitious son.

'All are with me, Father. Take your prodigal, turn him back –
for he will never submit come home –
or surrender your crown and consign to me.'
The ranges of dominions, of cherubs and seraphs
horde behind the Right Hand, solemn nodding.
God, an abandoned thing, Gloucester on the cliffs,
Raises his chin and refuses. 'I will end it
my way. I will see him
and he me
and reconcile ourselves. He does not mean

these things
with the tincture you read.'
The father took his keys and left
all cloud-borne children locked indoors
for him, alone, to face the terrible infant.

Now, returned
from this most late communication
unreceived, Gloucester waits
outside the gates
he built with his own mind. Ornate,
gaudy, embellished by the dedication
of slave labour seeking a better existence
beyond the possibility of all the life they live; surrenderers,
penitents, dedications from the mouths
of their babies and themselves
to adorn this fortress the father himself
controls no longer.
The shining son at the crenellation, watching,
allows him enter in rags.

The hosts of heaven decamp to kill Satan

Swarms of winged things, succulent babies
on flocculent pins, elderly leviathans
towering, proud,
a mist of insectish, spiny jewelled scarabs,
faces divine, well-groomed, moving in syncopated
neat choreography,
sprint free Heaven, out gates and windows, across
garden rows, tracking Satan's scent to his rest
in a suburban hospital bed.
That invalid already faded, waif-like,

translucent and over-alert, waking sees
these legions of species
creeping around the room, perched on the ceiling, loom
at the bed,
axes ready and flaming swords in hand.
None move to strike, none come close
beyond some unseen dome, some shell,
uncertain to Lucifer of origin, yet clear
it holds back this tide of vindicators
out to spill his blood.

A conversation between Jesus & Raphael reviewing the field

'What prevents them?' the right hand questioned
his own lieutenant, the archangel Raphael spying at his side
those hosts on Earth converged on the deathbed
of Satan the penitent. 'Why don't they strike?'
'Some thing intervenes, we can guess what,
and they dare not cross that will.' The son of God
looked further afield 'And what of those,
I see faces I know, forms I consorted with
in recent aeons?'
The archangel lowered his head
'Those are lost to us. Through questionable methods
or indignant false principles, entreaties from the enemy
or loss of intellect. They are the ravaged savages we left too long,
the merciful when brutality required, the brutes who refused
to show restraint. Sprung claws and spikes or caught between,
they are no longer of us.'
The intersected one gazed from corps to corps
estimating at a glance. 'Fewer remain
loyal to God

than have come undone and fled? This cannot be.'
'It is, and yet, most go a third way – unwilling to live in Hell,
unwelcome here in Heaven. It is unclear what number would serve
should Beelzebub field an army.'
Uncertain, Jesus counted, divided and weighed,
resolved to speak to Satan.

God offers again to let Lucifer re-enter Heaven

Eliding again from wakeful sleep
to somnolent consciousness, Lucifer-bedridden
reflects on those visions, those devils and angels
who persist in his head
all his life.
Post-investigation, confidently he passes judgement –
all are unnecessary, adornments at the most. Even God
a stick figure, straw-man to scatter the carrion scavengers
of human fear
from picking off the weak, a piñata to beat and assuage our rage
without we make mistake.

Muttering these discoveries, pale
half-light, surprised by sudden compression of air,
a density to everything, slowing luminescence,
he knows he is with God once more.
'We have nothing more to discuss' said Lucifer. 'You are dead
to me.'
The voice of everything no longer thick
nor resonant, a strange shade of vapourousness, escaping air,
a seething most unsettling. 'Lucifer,
don't be a fool. Look at what you've wrought – do you
not see the world? Half the host of Heaven
linger, crepuscular, unable to see the light. Your

fiends in allegiance with the fires below
likewise empty out, lose enthusiasm
for the project you abandoned. You have changed
the world. And now you do not want it?'
'Want it or not, it is not mine to take
nor yours to give.'
The vacuum fibrillated like an over-wet dog
'No, it is not. It is contested. But you have done
what you were bid – survive as human, know limitation;
survived and learned and thought. You can come home.'
Ashamedly Lucifer yet swelled to consider
return. Horrified at that Pavlovian reflex, that will
to submit
for the sake of acceptance, he tore out his catheter,
sprayed refuse on the floor.
'You only offer this
because you can withhold it. I am no better
than I was a century ago. I am no pure being
and nor are you. You are everything, all-father, everything,
including all my flaws. In such a way, who then
are you to give forgiveness?
Your children, good and evil,
range about the Earth, ambush each other
and others also, frantic to fetishize
a simple bout for power.'
'Listen to me' the sibilant deity
breathed 'round him, bed lodged
in the oesophagus of the universe
'I can forgive, give repentance, acceptance
back in Heaven. No more pain. No more limitation.'
Satan suspecting the inflection and scansion
inhaled and raised his head. 'For what? You "can", but won't,
unless from me..? What?'
Lucifer knew. Submission.
'Drive those mongrels of your now-repented treason,
destroy or imprison them,

contest the field for me. Do this,
and we will all retire to the sky,
resume what should have been. Replace
the replacements.'
Lucifer looked through bluish lids,
the room distorted by a haze of hubris.
'And then? Reset what you built
so we can sit at your feet and sing again
your greatness?
You don't want Armageddon. You prefer
this vile hierarchy, father pouting on his golden
throne, children bickering for attention.' God assailed
a vicious toothless roar, and Satan cringed
not: 'You are afraid?
Of what? With me not in Heaven, the devils remain in Hell.
What then can touch you?
Why seek me for your right hand
when you already have one?
Our stories are different; say it is Jesus
who may be vanquished,
say it cannot be a sure thing
unless God never created the universe in the first.
Then I will consider taking the field.'
The creator contracted, expelled dissatisfaction, refusal to speak.
'You are angry, but afraid? Where did you go,
from here? After last imposing on me? Angered
at my refusal,
and, perhaps,
ashamed?
That must have been an awful thing,
begettor,
reclusing as a failure,
crawling under your own front door
with no song in your voice
nor ears to hear it. Alone,
abandoned by your children. Did they see

through you?'
God flew to rage, revealing his face, seething vacuum
exploding in impotent fame.
'Do this thing, I command you!'
the voice again, not exact, but kin
to what Lucifer knew of old.
'Who are you? You pace like a panther
buried in a cage. Toothless,
no God of old. Enraged,
enfeebled. Strung. Who pulls
your strings?'
The sibilance subsumed, expanded,
suction disrupting the remnants
of Lucifer's frail form,
pressing in skin, mushing skull
and bones.
Masticated gum, Lucifer compressed,
on edge of exiting mortal life,
the splits in his being inlet memory
of all he had ever been.
The crimes and lies, the high mind
and fixed disdain,
and all before – the work he wrought in service to God,
his own remorse
and dutiful repentance. Remained: the life
so fleet, a blink,
wet and screaming grown soft and contemplative,
the family, deceit in friendship,
murder. He knew himself
as good as any other
borne by the flaws of creation. 'On balance, I say:
go away from me. I do not want it.
I reject Hell; I reject Heaven; I reject you. You, the timeless
dictator, insinuating your rules
in every thing, you who could make all right
if only you did not delight in building-in cracks

so that you might turn your back and despair
of all who fail the standards you never live to yourself.'
The room silent,
Satan expiring, drips of liquid
from a cheap space bag.
The ruined corpse rolled his head again
and saw God, already gone.

Satan expires

Lucifer, human, that mortal man limited perceiving
to the eyes and mind of one lone soul,
expired in a vapour of midges and starlight.
Luminosity collapsing, re-enfolding 'round his frail
shape, unremorseful in rejection
of the offers of God, the cajoling of Jesus.
Eternity dare not breathe as the prodigal following
that obliquitous path
comes to rest on the final groove, that rail laid by the creator
to channel Satan back to Heaven. Elements
gather themselves, turn, compress,
exit.

Book V - the final battle

Book V argument
Satan reemergent as purgatorial angel, meets a rogue empyrean survivor in what is left of Earth. The desolate mudball now serves as purgatory, humanity near-entirely relegated to oblivion, angels, infernals and inbetweeners roaming freely, hunting, battling, seeking to survive. The wandering defrocked angel tells Lucifer many things: how Beelzebub has died with indignity, and God's depleted force hunts down devils, angels, humans all for any slight.

Lucifer discovers a vast army come for him to be God and a small posse. God, now a shadow puppet for Jesus, roams the limbo of the world. Continents have decayed and sunk while Satan waited to awaken from death. Now fully cognate of all he has done in both lives, he looks about the Earth and sees a wasteland, where barely an angel or demon survives, and very few humans. Lucifer, refusing join battle for either side, is slain predicting Jesus' end as lonely imperfect perfectionist. The song of God destroys all imperfections, resulting in nothing but himself, a failure who unsays the world in hopes of recovering what was judged too harshly.

A squad of derelict, renegade angels, over-vigilantes, attacks a demonic outpost

Open plains, wasted fields,
two empyreans fidget at the peak, monstrous
volcanic outcrop recently impelled by some other
band of miscreants. Those angels batter, glue and nail
a thing of steel, one thousand other unnatural
components, filled with over-living essence
of all their zeal.
A third compatriot stands at the ledge,
observer of canyons, plateaus, mud-strewn flats below.
'They are there, creep out' he cries. A scream shrieks out,
the box rocks where they beat it, the imprisoned infernal caged
to drive it
shudders, wails some more.
'Die down!' demands one cherub, striving a spike in the side,
machine settled.
'How many do you see?'
The seraph at the eyrie craned, squinted and stared:
'The most – some fifteen, all the vile lot
we've run against ten years or more.' The crew on the mount
nod and agree, fire up their construction and pitch it off the cliff
as they fly straight
up, away, as fast as they can make.

The concoction imprisoning
some destitute fiend
plummets
drops,
exploding in the midst of a convocation of demon folk.
Many blasted sideways, most disintegrate,
the shockwave fells the mountainside
and levels an opposing range. The blast's breeze spreads
a warm breath the length of the continent,
grey mud everywhere; at long, long intervals

blinking people sneak out to see, swiftly
dart back within their rocks,
no food, no fortune,
blanket themselves once more in mud
for what comfort that delivers.

Lucifer re-emerges in the world, an empyrean in Purgatory; meets a forlost angel-storyteller

The night above this wasteland-Earth, inhabited,
deranged angels and grovelling devils, random humans laying
in refuse, tepid middens of filth; one star
shines,
the light re-emergent, oscillation in haze of radiation. The crisping
    work
scatters to Earth in sparks,
all extinguished before landfall
but for one.

Unfoldent in that still-burnful nick
where the largest smoulder fell,
Lucifer rose and flexed himself.
Wings outspread he flinched, bewondered.
Reaching up he touch the keel, finger slim
along the length. Gripping the shoulder
he tore them down and threw them in the mud.

'Be careful, Satan. You have no home,
no hearth fire to rekindle your innards
once you fall and fail and die.' The speaker
behind him, thin and withered,
fluttered his own emaciated wings.
'Ithuriel. It would seem your rage exhausts itself.'

The angel looked across the landscape,
contemplative.
'I too am lost. Jesus will come
soon, I am certain,
and then I die.'
'What is this place?' Lucifer stood carefully,
lightening at the edge of the world,
the air hot and dry,
underfoot everything thick and wet.
'Earth. You have come to Earth, light-bearer,
and still we are in darkness.
The world is being purged before the rapture.'

'Since Lucifer-human died, pandemonium
upsurged to Earth, Beelzebub rode out
and scoured all he could.
Bestrode a glorious, overwrought stallion,
resplendent in detailed finery,
gold armour, glass beading,
tassles and meringues, your lieutenant smiled to himself
and declared his war with God.
"What reason" said he "does God have oppose us,
except prevent our
reclamation of Satan?"' Ithuriel coughed.
'He gave many speeches,
railed and decryant, while angels and devils fell all over Earth,
rolling across mountains,
demolishing cities in their derbies.'
Ithuriel stepped walking, Lucifer keeping
pace. 'What of those warriors now?' asked Satan.
'Jesus has remained on high but the lord of the flies is dead' Ithuriel
showed no colour.
'Fell from his horse in this river of shit' – at
their feet a stream barely deep to the knee,
hardly wider than a horse long. Lucifer incredulous,
the angel-guide spoke on: 'The armour he wore – magnificent, ornate,

was most deathly weightful and awkward against mobility.
Unable to rise, Beelzebub drowned on his knees as the effluent
    flowed,
howling for his servants, standing, watched on
as his mouth and lungs all filled. I believe he
is down there still.' Lucifer saw only
a reflection of himself
in the surface of the slow-flowing ooze.

The morning star cast across the sea
of mud, horizon to horizon bare spires ejecting
through pools, craters, pits and vesicles,
rivers rolling all around.
'Beelzebub did this?' incredulous,
the reconstituted Lucifer,
noble, knowing all, remembrance
of everything and practice of his past,
held the world in disbelief.
'Not all' said Ithuriel. 'Not much.
This is God's work.'

That same angel goes on to tell that God has purged the Earth

'This Earth-now-purgatory is home to none – God's mobs roam
with scaffolds and hooks
to hang and quarter any devil or angel or human being they find
wanting. The number of angels is fewer every day.'
'And yet you wait for them?'
'I am certain I have sinned, and they will find me
frail.
But no, I remain because I am safe, happy here – beneath
my boulder, my stream is clean and my cave is warm.

I am safe beyond compare, should you meet another cherub
or denizen out there, all would crave what I possess.' And he flocked
back to his rock in the bog, perched and observed
the morning star.
'Do not linger,' said he,
and Satan left.

An army approaches Satan

Lucifer abandoned Ithuriel
to his boulder, stream
and cave beneath,
a great cloud sprayed to the sky at the horizon.
Before him, geysers of pestilent mud, an army riding
toward Satan.

As they drew close the morning star
perceived that battalion numbered far fewer than first thought.
Leading at a pace, the lord God himself
like a bandalero, raised his hand
and the archangels, dominions, a dozen ranged
on either side, drew up short, racing on all fours.
'Satan no longer, the prodigal emerged, prepared
for purgatoria!' The cheer of zealous, long-run servants
crowed about the waste.
'Look around you, lord' Satan waved and gestured. 'What
is this place you bring me to? No populace, nor birds nor trees,
a lake of steaming muck
and rarely a rock to stand on. What have you come to?'

He meets God but sees the disguise immediately

At each piece of speech Lucifer sees God flinch,
his entirety shimmer though lips remain still
however much he speaks.
'The world is renewed, light bearer. All wastrels
are destroyed, all
recalcitrant recidivist sinners spent.
all that remains are the anarchists of Hell, those
true lords of Heaven – a minor few
at most – and you, Lucifer.'
The lisping mimicry
of ill-formed ventriloquy
cored and jarred Satan's bones.
'What ridiculousness is this?' The crowd around him
unwilling pursue or question, he cast about,
turned back to God. 'I call it plain:
You are not God.' The angels raged
at apostasy.
'Fools! This is not God and never was! You
are Joshua ben Joseph, Jesus,
and wear our father's face like a mask?
What monstrous need be this?'
The eyes behind the lifeless face switched
uneasily.
'Lucifer, be silent. You do no useful
thing
with these sordid accusations.'
'You are Jesus! I know your beard.
Your sandals, too, betray
your failed imagination.
You visited me in hospital
and your stench remains the same.'
The son of God tore away his dead skin mask
and threw it on the ground. 'For what
do you do this, Lucifer? I *am* God; I am

the word, the truth and the life; I am
the father, the only son, the spirit too.
I will do what I will
and it shall be righteous!'

Many neighbouring dominions stepped
outward from the pair, slight murmurings; their
contraparts sensed apprehension, drew
flaming swords.
Like emitted positions in megahertz
the rush to arms called in the hordes
lingering in the swamp. A flock
of malingering demon-wings, cherubs forgotten
by God, mobs of half-lynched, rope
still dangling from long-stretched necks,
others adorned throughout their form
with pins and spikes inserted for ordeal,
and all the rest suffering
in the poisoned Earth around,
clambered to watch the battle brewing, to slake
their own violent urge.

Satan restocked his mind's context
for all the world around him: demons creeping,
seraphim poised, anger,
hatred,
all eyes on him and the governing Messiah.
Drool empooled in fangful craws,
feathered bullies weighed clubs and swords. The
packs divided, recombined, recalling as they
went
the deceit of Satan, the severity of Jesus
and His self-righteousness,
unforgiving contempt for compassion
misplaced or not.
Jesus noted them not.

'What do you want, Satan?' the son of God,
now patricide,
threw out his arms and gestured.
'Forget God; forget your chance at Heaven –
you were always to be found
wanting, whoever the judge may be.
Get gone.'
Lucifer looked around the throngs, small humans
holding crucifixes
to unclothed, filth-ridden bodies,
battered angels subdued, ever-loyal,
the slavering fangs of Hell... The feral nephilim
in between, those born lately
of the miscegenation precipitated by Satan's flight
and hibernation, sojourn.
'Gone where, dutiful one? Gone
where,
observant child? You are all
now
and all is wanting, lacks for flaws
introduced
by perfectionism
seeking cracks to criticise.
You are God? Then you made this' he gestured
at the broken horizon. 'You are all
and you are flaws, you are failure
too.'
'I am perfection!' the three-in-one
flared, rose and grew, exploding
bloom, magnificent,
imperious tree in a field of dandelions.

Lucifer defies Jesus

Satan pressed his chest at Jesus, the Earth around them,
vast field, sludge-filled,
craters and sticks, mutated rats and many legged cockroaches,
stretched monotony to the horizon.
The remnant armies of Heaven and Hell bestir,
sensing endful battle. The snarling hordes
bite and jibe, quickest amongst them
swift to strike, long-held grudges, short-fuse
fires,
their slow feet slough mud
to bring the violent orgy.
'You think yourself superior yet' Jesus drew his sword
'Lucifer, you most despicable betrayer,
come to us all with innocence on your tongue
and pride in your eyes. You who have lied
and incriminated at every turn, you
who should regret your own existence,
pose with pride at the shame you now feign.'
Lucifer watched the flaming blade
pace between them in the crucified's hand.
'Yes, son of God, I remorse
for all I did since the fall, before born human.
Also,
I remorse at serving our father so thoughtlessly;
what waste, what facile self-admiration, and I the lowly mirror
for him to pose and preen.
Far better my so-short life on Earth, a child,
an adult, ageing into death. I do not regret,
except that one crime which I know I fell to in weakness,
flaw installed by God himself and exploited by his minions.
But the knowledge of life lived, the memory
and living scenes inside my head
go with me, wherever I will be.'
'You will be nowhere once you die here' spake the Messiah.

'But I was, and so ever I shall be. My life is not undone,
and once it is passed it never can
not be. Forever upon the eternal record, irremovable trace,
whatever goes from here. And it was lived; and it had meaning.
Your story has not played out. You are king of all, but all
of which you are king
is a bog and many corpses.'
As Satan spake, the many angels clawing faces
of demons, fiends about them
sank into morass, their final spurs of energy spent
bringing their siblings down.

Jesus and Lucifer confront one another

'You would fight me?' Jesus stamped and surged.
'I am the Konami code, deus ex deo,
no machine necessary.
You hate our love, Satan, you
hate our way of life, always have.'
'I hate your hypocrisy, sententious sophist!
You killed our father and wear his face for a mask,
like a wishful child,
and you speak of "love"!'

'I am love, Satan, I am light. Whatever
I am, whatever I choose to be, that is "love". You
are my enemy, you are not me. You are not love.'
Jesus raised his weapon and rained redemption
on Lucifer.

Satan staggered crabwards, returned upright
to speak: 'How can you adorn for war,
when love was always your catch-cry?' 'Long

before I had my own mind (a laugh aside
at how fraught the thought, gauntlet of solipsism
yawning before him eternally) – long before I had a slogan,
I already had a purpose.
I am here to destroy Satan. That is why
I was born in the thoughts of my father-mother-
cousin-brother-self. The kernel of my being is revenge.
What would you do, for such a situation?
The object of my existence exited his prison-home,
unprotected,
making pretence to replace me?
I needs must play the role
the people all wrote for me. Those haughty words
attributed, become my mantle and my gloves.
The claims to superhumanity self-fulfil
whether I want or not.'
Turning to the miserable faithful surrounding them in throng: 'I am
he of whom you've spoken, and I have no other role.
Let us cleanse this Earth,
that we may live in Paradise.'

Jesus strikes Satan again; mocks poesis

Again the son swung his blade
and Lucifer-no-longer-human
fell,
gaped, staggered and restood.
'Are you not a poet?' the son sneered
'A writer-creator?
Accomplished manipulator of phrase and saying, charm?
Why not save yourself
with a chariot spoken to life? Why not
arm thyself

with the sword thy pen
and strike me down with well-shaped lines
that fly and pierce like a javelin?'
Seeping Satan grinned: 'Jesus, you are a fool.
A poet is not one
to labour greatly and in time be master
of all the terms in the world. A poet is servant
to verbs, venerator of adjectives,
worshipper of words. I do not
crack a whip, insist my lines play nice,
roll over. They lead me to throw myself through fire,
they give me kind moments after long
humble submission. They are my family,
co-conspirators, my mystics. But never
servants. They may bend
and I may twist
but purpose is never a shaped thing with them; they do the shaping
I the shaped.
Jesus, you are a fool. You are not the word,
you are not the way. You are a fiction unto yourself
and your life is lost to us, almost.
What can you teach that has not been
obliterated, obfuscated,
or reformed in other words?
Jesus, you are a fool.

In your quest for perfection, who is left? Who amongst
your "many faithful" has no flaw?'
Lucifer defiant, stood and set his feet,
declaimed Christ's plan for Armageddon: 'Perfectionist
eliminating perceived imperfections,
you'll boil off virtue
in your quest to sterilise the world.
Smash and attack, lance eruptions, inconvenient
questions. And at the end
the entire world is destroyed, Jesus left

with no one and no thing to rule since
no one is perfect, the only people who believe in you
revealed molesters, absconders,
and so you'll kill them too. Lucifer dies,
the angels all die, Jesus sits in a bog of nothing
and grins at his own winning. Is that it? The concrete ball,
a sphere so neat, unambiguously screed and floated,
impervious and ageless. The world so perfect now.
A monument for Jesus to pace eternally, cement walk
of his solution, achievement.'

As the angels question their allegiance, Beelzebub reappears, poor inflated bag

One then another of the grappling empyreans
twisted an eye to observe Jesus, comprehend
where their allegiance leads them.
'Don't' cautioned the son of God,
and many yet resumed obedience, like
pets that fear the cold.
Yet several and more saw wisdom in Lucifer's
words, searing quickly the thought
that all would cease once Jesus had installed
utter silence, unending.

Amidst sick-making quiet, eyed
stand-off between, across
fraternal lines, an osculant wetness announced the presence
of one more protagonist.
That flapping compost, the pig-king of Hell,
clambered as an entertainer across the mud like a duck.
'Listen to Lucifer! Jesus is wrong! He seeks destroy us all!'
The eyes unseeing in his hollow head, hideous wounds,

beneath a mouth oozed of ebullient muck.
The least dignified, most unseemly venal beasts
amongst the multitude recoiled no less
than the delicate cherubs
eviscerating their foes, to see the spectacle
of that sewer-filled form flop boneless up the beach
imploring more to his cause.
Momentarily unified by common horror
the forces on all sides turned blades towards Bael;
yet of the two, Jesus' promise
of ceased existence
perturbed more than that gormless mess.
The hellish and
heavenly
in desperate desire to flee the parricide
rushed to join the lord of the flies.

Many angels resolve to serve with Hell, prevent Armageddon

The angels – too late – sided with Beelzebub, bid
prevent Armageddon, that they might continue existence.
Lieutenants and dominions argued every point –
who commands whom,
the colour their uniforms, the standard calibre
for all their infernal weapons –
and Jesus cleaned up the survivors, striking, smiting,
tsunami-shaped his flaming blade
swept the many away. Reinflated,
Beelzebub's hollow corpse once more
arose, gestured with a smile 'Behold, I am risen and go before thee.
Do not despair!'
The son of God smote down that toad's throat, yet again

it flowered and bloomed.
'To hell with him' said Jesus, and turned once more to Lucifer.
Sneaking pantomime, the toothless pig-king
wavered, cajoling,
staggered to shake off the blow.
Animated from within by some frivolous demon,
the shredded head fell off
and Furcifer's face emerged,
bloodied, ichoric, split and failing.
'We had some fun, didn't we?' he smiled fading,
dusty weeds dispersed on the wind.

The last fall on Lucifer and each other, stabbing and beating

Those remnants of Hell, fledglings of purgatory,
disintegrating, dissipated by the savagery of Jesus,
wounded unrising ever, still aflame
with resentful hate at all Satan brought on them,
turned once more, clawing their last to besmirch the prodigal,
thorny mass falling one on another,
flailing to the last.
And amongst them Lucifer fell. Hated
by all, dismayed at everything. Jesus thrust his spear
at that most hated elder brother, headless Beelzebub-balloon beside
    him
conjoined in spiteful rage. Raphael sought
spleen Lucifer upon a rock,
show his master dedication to the job was far from gone,
spite outlasting final breaths.

The end. Jesus unsays the world

'You are a flaw, Light-bearer; an error.
Your mistake was being born, created
at all. Your existence is a blemish
on my father's perfection, your remorse nothing
but a corruption of the penitent. Your
voice dischords the songs of the worshippers,
your form mis-shapes the eye.
You must be gone.'
Satan's remaining baleful eye rolled out
its stalk
atop a catastrophised head,
ambrosial innards reeking his face,
semblance of survival long surrendered.
Every degree within all orbit
heavenly beings and fallen watchers, siblings
long estranged,
lay destroyed, bitter and rapacious, neglected, thwarted,
done.
'None are left to worship you, Christ, for none
meet your desired perfection. The only perfect thing
is flawless; featureless; smooth and unremarkable;
unworthy, not worth living.
You have reduced the Earth, now eternal,
to a faceless ball of no conclusion, no beginning. A smooth mousse
of decayed organelles, unable to rise or recompose.
And now there is only you. What next, Word of God?
Every thing you say
advances this embalmment, this over-polishing renders
non-existent
what you thought to preserve and improve;
to rule.
All left you is the act of being
you, of speaking and saying these things
that bring about the failure of everything that waited here for you.'

Jesus stared down Lucifer, dying, 'There is no conclusion', refusing
to speak, ceasing to exist. 'I see' said Lucifer 'You
regret.'
Jesus sought no more world – a thing flawed when flaws breed
    dissent –
by saying no more, the anti-word, unspeaking all creation,
the crucified one sucking words reversed, spoken backwards,
breathed inwards, inhaling, absorbed like toxic fumes
assimilated to his flesh... Jesus chanted the days, the nights,
the swine and trees, brutality bleak winter food all monuments and
    human talk, seas and oceans, creatures undiscovered to human
    eyes,
teeming fleets of mites and larks, Roc, Leviathan, frequencies and
    wavelengths
yet to be measured, holes in thought and chlorophyll,
absorbed it all, unsaying, denied, lied that it ever was. And so it wasn't.

Lucifer and Christ across a puddle of phosphorous,
glowing residue of boiled off excrement. The face of Christ
on the air in his mouth, head reversing inside out, black obelisk
stretched thin and soft, the wings of nothing as the serpent who
    swallows itself. 'Ouroboros, you are no more.'
Jesus inhaling cannot stop saying the world backwards, in frantic
    reflex
coughed to resay everything, restore the trees, bring back the sun.
Air and mud infilled his face, corpses and weapons, maggot-ridden
feet, the stones of the Earth and vapour of the air, all drawn in
to his enormous unhinged jaw, a thing he cannot stop unsaying until
he unsays himself, the word reversed and swallowed to a dot.

And Satan's name was unsaid but remains, the eternal record
    irremovable from being something that always will be having
    been.

Lucifer gathered what was left, and invited a language to speak of itself.